Classroom Activities
in Japanese Culture and Society

Wisconsin Department of Public Instruction
Herbert J. Grover, State Superintendent

Lloyd H. Joyal and Miriam B. Hansen

Japan Program Services
Center for International Education
University of Wisconsin-Eau Claire

Robert H. Gomoll
Director
Bureau for Program Development

Frank M. Grittner
Supervisor
Foreign Language Education

This publication is available from:

Publication Sales
Wisconsin Department of Public Instruction
P.O. Box 7841
Madison, WI 53707-7841
(608) 266-2188

Bulletin No. 0340

Copyright © 1990 by Wisconsin Department of Public Instruction

Contents

Foreword

In 1987, the State Superintendent's Advisory Council for Japanese Language and Culture submitted a report to Governor Tommy Thompson. One of the Advisory Council committees prepared a series of "Recommendations on Enhancing Instruction in Japanese History and Culture." *Classroom Activities in Japanese Culture and Society* fulfills the recommendation that the "Department of Public Instruction develop a publication on materials and resources related to the study of Japan."

This guide provides valuable background material on the history, geography, educational system, and everyday life of Japanese people. The material is organized so that elementary and secondary teachers can readily draw from it to enhance their regular classroom instruction. Furthermore, the large number of graphs, figures, and maps can be transformed quickly into handouts and transparencies for direct use with students. Finally, the list of resources on Japan is extensive and current, thus enabling teachers to go far beyond the scope of the curriculum supplement itself.

As noted in the DPI *Guide to Curriculum Planning in Social Studies*, (Bulletin no. 6751, 1986), we must study Japan and other nations to see the global picture. We have neglected Japan and other Asian Rim nations in past programs. Therefore, it is fully appropriate that we provide special assistance to teachers so they can give their students an accurate and current view of Japan and its people. This guide will prove useful in achieving that end.

Herbert J. Grover
State Superintendent

Preface

Once symbolized by cherry blossoms and Mount Fuji, Japan has become known in recent years for its cameras, electronic equipment, and automobiles. We are only beginning to appreciate the tremendous strides Japan has made in postwar rehabilitation and continuing industrial expansion.

The United States clearly is affected by what Japan makes, buys, and sells today. Many Japanese citizens have been very successful students and have achieved high recognition in Western societies. Numerous Japanese companies have made substantial investments in the United States, and thousands of Americans owe their livelihood to Japan's continued economic success.

Americans need to understand the tremendous national energy evident in contemporary Japan. This increasing activity has made elementary and secondary students more aware of Japan and has heightened their interest in this important country.

This guide is designed to provide informational foundations in the history, geography, society, and culture of Japan. It is intended as a source book for teachers and administrators who would like to improve the curricular offerings and understandings regarding our Far East neighbor. The background information, lesson plans at the elementary and secondary levels, and extensive bibliography should prove helpful for curriculum development or revision.

Impetus for the guide's development came from a group of Wisconsin citizens appointed to the State Superintendent's Advisory Council for Japanese Language and Culture in 1986. Japan Program Services at UW-Eau Claire assumed the responsibility for developing a guide for Wisconsin educators. Through the able assistance of many individuals, especially Miriam Hansen, Hiroyuki Toyota, and Frank Grittner, this collection of teaching ideas was developed.

Support for development of the visuals included in this guide came from a special grant from the UWEC Office of the Dean of Graduate Studies. They were produced by the UWEC Media Development Center.

We believe that the classroom teacher is the most important link to helping students understand other peoples and cultures. We hope that this guide will improve these global understandings in Wisconsin classrooms and elsewhere.

Lloyd H. Joyal, Ph.D.
Coordinator, Japan Program Services
Center for International Education
University of Wisconsin-Eau Claire

Acknowledgments

When one completes a project of this nature, it is done so with the realization that many others have provided help.

Lloyd Joyal, coordinator of Japan Program Services at the University of Wisconsin-Eau Claire, and Frank Grittner, foreign language consultant for the Wisconsin Department of Public Instruction, initiated this project.

I wish to express special gratitude to Hiroyuki Toyota, assistant coordinator of Japan Program Services at the University of Wisconsin-Eau Claire, who offered many helpful suggestions as well as reviewing and editing this document.

Special thanks to those Wisconsin educators who have contributed ideas and lesson plans, reviewed, revised, and encouraged: Charlotte Myhers, Beth Elver, Jerry Johnson, Betty Cowley, Pat Wassink, Sally-Jo Michalko, Hilary Stock, and Sally Henshaw.

Several student typists and office workers also have contributed to this publication, and their efforts are appreciated: Debbie Gilbertson, Brian Ganje, Julie Rohrer, and Matt Goetz.

The staff of the Center for International Education at UW-Eau Claire was extremely supportive. Thanks especially to Kathy Krebsbach, Sue Klink, and Linda Wood.

Finally, a word of thanks goes to everyone at the DPI who shaped this book into its final form: text editors Michele Gale-Sinex, Denise Starkey, and Paul Zelewsky, graphic artists Vicki Rettenmund, Dianne Larnutzer, and Neldine Nichols, and proofreaders Jennifer Vogelgesang, Sandy Roethler, and Lisa Isgitt. The Word Processing Center also deserves sincere thanks for its patience and accuracy, especially Sandra House, Deb Motiff, and Danni Jorenby.

Miriam Hansen
University of Wisconsin-Eau Claire

This book attempts to make close connections with the social studies topics and concepts found in *A Guide to Curriculum Planning in Social Studies*, published by the Wisconsin Department of Public Instruction in 1986. To fulfill this goal, the authors have compiled background information, lessons and activities, and resources for Wisconsin teachers. The following social studies topics have been selected for their relevance to the study of Japan.

Elementary Level: Topics

What are families like in other parts of the world?

How do people in other parts of the world celebrate their holidays?

How do geographic features influence the way we live?

Who settled our community?

How do people in our community make a living?

What problems might a person from another culture have in adjusting to a community in which another language is spoken?

How do farming methods compare in different parts of the world?

What does our community do to contribute to other parts of the world?

What problems are common to most communities? What is being done to find solutions?

How have different environments affected the way people live in different regions of the world?

How are the components of our culture (that is, education, religion, literature, and arts) reflected in our communities?

In what ways are Wisconsin and Japan linked to one another?

Intermediate Level: Topics

What factors shape cultures?

How can people from other cultures understand me without speaking my language?

How can cultures be compared?

How have cultural regions changed over time?

What changes might occur in the future? How will these changes affect us?

What role does technology play in cultural change?

How are nations becoming more interdependent?

What happens when cultures conflict?

How can conflicts between nations be resolved or avoided?

How is the future of the United States tied to the future of the world?

Who immigrated to the United States? How has the United States received them?

What are some of the contributions made by immigrants to the United States?

How have U. S. citizens been affected by the country's relationship with the rest of the world?

What changes and challenges has the United States faced in the twentieth century? Which ones might be faced in the twenty-first century?

Secondary Level: Topics

How did nationalism, industrialism, imperialism, and militarism bring change to the United States, Europe, and Asia?

How has geography influenced the history and economic development of Asia?

How do art, literature, folklore, and religion reflect Asian cultural values?

Why has Asia been considered a cultural crossroads?

How have the political and economic interests of European nations and the United States influenced the course of Asian history?

What are some important contributions of Asian nations to the world?

How did the United States expand its interests and involvement around the world?

How did earlier American policies of isolation and neutrality influence events in Asia?

What were the arguments for and against using the atomic bomb in World War II? What are the arguments for and against its use today?

What role has the United States taken in Asia since World War I?

How will the United States respond to the demands of minority groups to achieve equality of opportunity?

How are our communities examples of global interdependence?

How has technology changed the way Americans relate to each other, the land, and the world?

How have economic and business cycles affected Americans?

What roles should the United States be playing in world affairs?

How have increasing interdependence and instant communication affected the economy and world affairs?

What relationships exist between United States foreign policy and economic well-being?

Because of its broad scope, social studies reaches far beyond the covers of the classroom textbook. The Japan-United States Textbook Study Project conducted in 1981 by the National Council of Social Studies and the Embassy of Japan pointed to the need for more inclusive information in the Japanese and the U. S. textbooks about each other's countries. More controversial topics, the report pointed out, should not be avoided, and more attention should be given to differing points of view. Current material should be included and sources of information should be identified. Social, political, and economic events, as well as cultural and artistic developments, should have fuller coverage. Even though textbook publishers are attempting to meet these suggestions, they face limits on the number of pages and the weight of a textbook.

To go beyond the range of information that can reasonably be covered in a text and to provide background material where there are omissions in texts, the authors have attempted to present a few lesson plans. Each lesson states some of the broad concepts expressed in the Wisconsin *Guide to Curriculum Planning in Social Studies*. As a rule, these concepts directly relate to a level of instruction—elementary, intermediate, or secondary. After the lesson's title come specific objectives. For each lesson, these statements were designed to provide an overview rather than an all-inclusive range of topics. The authors have tried to limit them to a manageable number.

Creating a "Discovery Box"

This idea was contributed by Sally-Jo Michalko, Meadowbrook Elementary, 3130 Rolling Ridge, Waukesha, WI 53188.

An extremely effective way to enliven the classroom study of another culture is the "Discovery Box". A Discovery Box is a box filled with cultural artifacts accompanied by student activities. In selecting items for the box, it is important that a balance be maintained between traditional and contemporary daily use items to guard against the perpetuation of stereotypes.

The following are some ideas for starting a collection of artifacts.

I. **Language**
   A. American and Japanese newspapers
   B. Familiar children's storybooks (such as *Cinderella, The Three Bears, Jack and the Beanstalk*). As you show the pictures, have someone describe what's happening in the pictures. Emphasize that the printed word stands for the spoken word.
   C. Books and tapes
   D. Textbooks
   E. Make cards for the Language Master machine (your teacher of the learning disabled or speech therapist may have one). The cards can have the foreign word printed on the front with your voice pronouncing the new word on the tape. The students can practice the new language by repeating after you.

II. **Music**
   A. Traditional music
   B. Contemporary music
   C. Rock star posters
   D. Toy instruments

III. **Food**
   A. Cookbooks: Try a cooking experience with your students.
   B. Child's lunchbox

IV. **Stamps**

V. **Money**

VI. **Art**
   A. Samples of student artwork
   B. Pictures of artisans working
   C. Paintings, drawings, sculptures, pottery, weaving

VII. **Physical Education**
      A. Games
      B. Teach the students to count to ten.
          1. Use this for numbering off teams
          2. Use for counting while doing exercises
      C. Dances

VIII. **Toys**

IX. **Resources**
     Obviously, the easiest way to collect artifacts is through foreign travel, but if that's not possible, contact the following resources for posters, pamphlets, newspapers, magazines, foods, etc.:
     A. Airlines
     B. Consulates
     C. Embassies
     D. Travel agencies
     E. Traveling friends and colleagues
     F. Specialty product stores (import stores, ethnic grocery stores)
     G. Local Chamber of Commerce (inquire about businesses that export products from your community, and foreign companies located in your area)

Learning about another culture through the "Discovery Box" technique has motivated my students to want to learn about more people who make up our global community. The students progress from thinking about themselves in the context of their immediate surroundings to thinking about themselves in the context of the world.

History and Geography

1

Historical Overview

Little is known of Japan's history prior to the fourth century. From 10,000 years ago until the third or second century B.C., referred to as the Jomon Period, its people mainly hunted and fished. According to a legend from this period, Jinmu Tenno, the first emperor of Japan, directly descended from the Sun Goddess Amaterasu. All subsequent emperors trace their ancestry to him, and, by extension, to Amaterasu.

The Yayoi Period followed the Jomon Period and lasted until approximately the third century A.D. During this time, the Japanese mastered the art of rice cultivation, began to use metal instruments, and established the fundamental patterns of Japanese life.

During the fourth century, when the Yamato Dynasty was established, Japan was unified as a state. At that time most people practiced Shintoism, a religion which features the worship of nature, ancestors, and ancient national heroes. The divinity of the emperor was Shintoism's major tenet.

A New Religion

Buddhism came to Japan from Korea during the sixth century. The Asian religion played an important role in the creation of Japanese culture.

Early in the seventh century, Prince-Regent Shotoku established a constitutional government. He also contributed much to the advancement of culture and education.

Prior to 710, the site of the capital was changed each time a new emperor took the throne. In 710 a permanent seat for the court was established at Nara, and the full-fledged Imperial Era began.

Buddhism flourished in this period as thousands of temples were constructed throughout the country. Sculptures and other fine art influenced by Buddhism appeared. Some of these works still exist today. The most impressive of these, a great bronze statue of the Buddha cast in 752, sits in the Todaiji Temple in Nara. This is the largest statue of the Buddha in Japan.

In 794 when Kyoto became the capital, Japan entered an era of prosperity, the Heian Period, which lasted until 1192.

During the Heian Period, the Japanese imported ideas and customs from China and Korea and blended them with their own culture. The invention of a new Japanese writing system, based on Chinese writing, brought about a flowering of literature and poetry. *The Tale of Genji*, written in the early eleventh century by Murasaki Shikibu, a woman of the nobility, was the world's first novel.

In the early stages of this period, the Imperial Court gained great power and enjoyed prosperity and glory. Later, however, military clans started a series of civil wars that pushed Japan into the feudal era.

Feudal Era

The Feudal Era began when Yoritomo, the head of the military Genji, established a shogunate government at Kamakura in 1192. During this period various sects of Buddhism developed. One sect, Zen, appealed to the warrior class. Zen life was simple yet vigorous, and its art and literature reflected this simplicity.

Historical Overview

A Timeline of Japanese History*

ca. 8000 – 300 B.C.	**Jomon Period**
	Hunting and fishing are the primary activities.
ca. 300 B.C. – ca. A.D. 300	**Yayoi Period**
	Rice cultivation and use of metal tools and earthenware pottery increase.
ca. 300 – 645	**Yamato Period**
552 or 538	Chinese writing is adapted. Buddhism is introduced.
593 – 622	Regency of Prince Shotoku begins.
600 – 784	**Nara Period**
607	First envoy from Japan visits China.
710	Capital moves to Nara.
752	Daibutsu Buddha is dedicated.
794 – 1185	**Heian Period**
794	Kyoto becomes the capital.
894	Fujiwara family gains control. Envoys to China are stopped.
ca. 1002 – 1019	*The Tale of Genji* is written. Taira family comes to power.
1185 – 1333	**Kamakura Period**
1192	Feudalism and Zen Buddhism emerge. Shogunate government is established.
1274	Mongols first invade.
1333	Shogunate falls.
1333 – 1573	**Ashikagao (Muromachi) Period**
	Wealthy class emerges and champions the arts, literature, tea ceremonies, and architecture.
1543	Portuguese arrive.
1549	Missionary Francis Xavier arrives.
1568 – 1603	**Momoyama Period**
1568	Civil wars end when Oda Nobunaga seizes Kyoto and tries to re-establish shogunate.
1582	Nobunaga is assassinated.
1590	Hideyoshi restores order.
1592	Japan invades Korea.

*Sources often vary on exact dates in early Japanese history, especially for historical periods.

1600 – 1868	**Edo Period**
1603	Tokugawa Shogunate begins in Edo.
1639	Country is closed to foreigners and merchant class grows.
1700	Tokyo (Edo) becomes capital city. Haiku poetry emerges.
1853	Commodore Perry arrives at Uraga.
1854	Treaty of Kanagawa opens trade with the United States.
1867	Shogunate falls, and Emperor Meiji comes to the throne.
1868 – 1912	**Meiji Period**
	Sovereignty is restored to the Emperor.
1876	The samurai lose power.
1894 – 1895	Sino-Japanese War
1904 – 1905	Russo-Japanese War
1912-1926	**Taisho Period**
1914	Japanese military grows. Japan declares war on Germany.
1923	Great Tokyo earthquake.
1926 – present	**Showa Period**
1926	Hirohito becomes emperor.
1940	Japan signs alliance with Germany.
December 7, 1941	Japan attacks Pearl Harbor.
1941 – 1945	World War II in Pacific
August 6 and 9, 1945	United States drops atomic bombs on Hiroshima and Nagasaki.
1945 – 1952	Allied forces occupy Japan.
1946	Japan adopts a democratic government.
1956	Japan joins the United Nations.
1974	President Gerald Ford visits Japan, the first visit by a U.S. president.
1980	Japan emerges as a leader in the World Market. Control of World Banks. Highest per capita income in the world.
1988	Death of Emperor Hirohito.

The shoguns led extravagant lives and prospered until the first half of the fifteenth century, when civil strife ravaged various parts of the country.

During these wars, which continued for more than a century, art and culture somehow managed to flourish. The *noh* drama, the tea ceremony, flower arranging, and landscape gardening gradually developed into the forms still seen today. Feudal lords also built majestic castles for defense as well as to show their power over the people.

Tokugawa Ieyasu's rise to power in 1603 established his government at Edo, present-day Tokyo. This government was able to keep the powerful local lords in check. Government strength is the main reason Japan flourished for the 260 years of the Edo Period.

In 1633 Tokugawa closed all the ports to international trade because the shogun disliked the effects of foreign influence on his country. The port of Nagasaki, however, remained open to the Dutch and Chinese. In this peaceful era Kabuki drama and woodblock prints became popular, and stone and porcelain ware, silk brocade, and lacquerware improved in quality.

Western Influence

During the mid-nineteenth century, a commercial economy and a modern urban culture emerged, after the influence of Commodore Perry of the U.S. Navy. Perry brought his fleet to the port of Uraga, near Tokyo, in 1853 and forced Japan to open trade with the United States. This sudden encounter with the West and its relatively advanced technology triggered the downfall of the Tokugawa Shogunate government. Japan found it necessary to catch up with the outside world. It was the advent of a new era.

By 1868 the Meiji Imperial Government was established in Tokyo as Japan set a course for rapid modernization. Western culture flowed into Japan at a quick pace, and the people quickly assimilated the new ways. Progress under the new constitutional government was remarkable. A postal system was set up; railway and shipping services were started; and the first airline company was established. Japan's industrial revolution, which had ended by the close of the Meiji Era, lasted only 45 years. Japan is now a highly developed industrial nation.

Isolated from the world for approximately 240 years, Japan created its own culture and traditions. Recently, the Japanese gradually have begun to adopt many Western ideas, in areas such as housing and diet. Despite the country's high population density, Japan maintains a high standard of sanitation and a low crime rate.

Notable Japanese

Names in this list are arranged chronologically. They appear by surname (family name), then first name; this is the normal order for Japanese names. No commas are used to separate the names, except where a title, such as emperor, is used.

Shotoku Taishi (?-621). Son of Emperor Yomei, Prince Shotoku Taishi brought Buddhism to Japan after assuring his father that it did not conflict with Shintoism. He also composed the country's first written laws, encouraged the spread of the arts, and encouraged the construction of a great number of temples. Many still revere him as the ancestral patron of carpenters.

Murasaki Shikibu (985-?). A woman of nobility and author of the world's first novel, *The Tale of Genji*. Murasaki wrote the 54-volume tale about aristocrats' lives and loves. Her novel provides insight into the Japanese culture of her time. Though little information about her personal life exists, many believe that Murasaki married a distant cousin, and had one daughter. Because she was widowed as a young woman around 1001, Murasaki became an attendant to the empress. Evidence in her writings indicates that she died between 1030 and 1040.

Minamoto Yoshitsune (1159-1189). A famous warrior in Japanese history and the younger half-brother of Minamoto Yoritomo, Minamoto established the first shogunate. He was raised by the Fujiwara family and learned the ways of noblemen and martial arts before joining his half-brother to defeat the Taira clan. His success as a general stirred his half-brother's suspicions about his ambitions and led to Yoshitsune's eventual forced suicide. His sad story has made him a legendary figure in literature.

Toyotomi Hideyoshi (1537-1598). Born a peasant and known as a very disruptive child, Toyotomi became one of the most powerful leaders of Japan. In 1586, Toyotomi built the Osaka castle that has become the focal point of commercial growth for modern Osaka, Japan's second largest city.

Tokugawa Ieyasu (1543-1616). Born to the Matsudaira family, Tokugawa's father gave him away as a hostage at age four. Soon after, he was captured by one of the powerful families. Tokugawa never saw his father again. Later he assumed leadership in the military and became shogun, establishing the last great feudal dynasty, the Tokugawa Shogunate. Even though he devoted much of his life to war, Tokugawa's system of government led to one of Japan's longest periods of unity, peace, and prosperity.

Takatoshi Hachirobei (1621-1694). A talented and successful merchant, Takatoshi used innovative business practices, selling at low, fixed prices for cash and advertising his large store in Edo. His monetary exchange system was the predecessor of the Mitsui Bank. His family business—led by six sons—continued to play a leading role in the industrial growth of Japan in the 1800s and continues today as one of the largest conglomerates in the world.

Matsuo Basho (1644-1694). Matsuo developed haiku poetry. One of his most famous works is *Shichi Bushu*, a collection composed by Matsuo and his ten disciples. In Japan his most famous work is *Okunohosomichi* (*The Narrow Road to the North*), which he wrote in 1694. Matsuo's given name was Kinsaku, but he adopted Basho (banana tree) when he moved into a hut with a banana tree nearby. He worked for a local lord who wrote poetry and, under the lord's influence, began to write.

Chikamatsu Monzaemon (1653-1724). Known as Japan's greatest playwright, Chikamatsu's writings rival Shakespeare's. He was born to a samurai family but chose Buddhism over fighting; later he became a writer. His works include plays written for the Bunraku puppet theater and for the Kabuki theater.

Ando Hiroshige (1797-1858). The most famous of Japan's woodblock print artists, Ando was born in Edo, the son of a Tokugawa Shogunate official. "Fifty-three Post Stations of the Tokkaido Road," a landscape painting, is his most recognized work. An orphan at age

12, Ando learned drawing from a fireman. Later, after he had studied with the artist Toyohiro, he changed his name from his given name Tokutaro to Hiroshige. He continued making prints and paintings of birds, flowers, and landscapes until 1858 when he died of cholera during an epidemic that swept through Edo.

Nakahama Manjiro (1826-1898). Born in a fishing village on Shikoku, Nakahama was pulled from the sea by an American whaling vessel in 1841 after he lost his fishing ship to a storm. Unable to return to Japan, Nakahama lived in Massachusetts, Hawaii, and California before returning to Japan as a translator with Commodore Perry. He continued to serve his country as a translator; he taught English, whaling, navigation, and published the first English-language phrase book, *Eibei Taiwa Shokei (A Shortcut to Anglo-American Conversation)*.

Iwasaki Yataro (1835-1885). Through both legal and illegal means, the founder of the Mitsubishi financial empire traded goods and cash, accumulating tremendous wealth. After entering the steamship business, he beat most of the competition by undercutting prices and starting longer shipping routes. He expanded into mining, banking, insurance, iron foundries, and other fields. Iwasaki's funeral, attended by 50,000 mourners, reflected his popularity.

Meiji, Emperor Mutsuhito (1852-1912). Meiji used the tenets of Shintoism to establish himself as a divine ruler when he became the 122nd emperor in 1868. After abolishing the samurai class system, he instigated reforms that led to turbulence but also opened Japan's diplomatic doors to the rest of the world. Meiji transformed Japan into a modern state. As a boy he loved to play war games with wooden swords and hobby horses, but reportedly fainted at the sound of gunshot in 1864.

Noguchi, Dr. Hideyo (1876-1928). Born to peasant parents, Noguchi studied medicine as a teen-ager by living at the home of a doctor and observing him. Noguchi went to school in Tokyo. In 1900 he came to the United States and studied bacteriology at the University of Pennsylvania. Later, while doing research at the Rockefeller Institute for Medical Research, he discovered the cause of syphilis. He contracted yellow fever on the African Gold Coast while trying to determine the cause of that disease and died from it in 1928.

Suzuki Shin'ichi (1898-   ). A well-known musician and creator of the Suzuki violin method, Suzuki had an early start in music, since his father built violins. After studying in Germany, he developed an educational program for the violin based on the premise that "anyone's talent can be developed through education." From the music school he opened in Nagano Prefecture, Suzuki's teaching method has spread all over the world.

Hirohito, Emperor Michi no Miya (1901-1988). The 124th and longest-reigning emperor of Japan, Hirohito was a recognized marine biologist and writer. Before World War II he traveled in Europe and was familiar with Western ways. He differed considerably from his predecessors, who were treated as living gods. His wife, Nagako (1903-   ) is an artist; his son, Emperor Akihito (1933-   ) studied politics and economics at Gakushuin University in Tokyo. Akihito, like his father, is the symbol of the state and according to the constitution, derives his position from the will of the people.

National Anthem

While it is not played as frequently as "The Star Spangled Banner" is in the United States, Japan's national anthem, "Kimigayo," ("The Reign of Our Emperor") is much older. The lyrics, taken from a Japanese *waka* poem over 1,000 years old, were first put to music in 1860 by British army bandmaster John William Fenton. Later, Hiromori Hayashi, a court musician, gave the anthem a new melody.

Kimi ga yo wa
Chiyo ni yachiyo ni
Sazareishi no
Iwao to nari te
Koke no musu made.

Ten thousand years of happy reign be thine
Rule on, my lord, till what are pebbles now
By ages united to mighty rocks shall grow
Whose venerable sides the moss doth line.
(translation B.H. Chamberlain)

National Flower

Since ancient times, *sakura no hana*, cherry blossoms, have been Japan's national flower. The fragile and short-lived blossoms symbolize resignation and a willingness to die for one's lord, qualities valued by the feudal samurai warriors.

As long ago as the tenth century, wealthy individuals had special stands built where they would celebrate spring by admiring and writing poetry about the cherry blossoms. Today, each April, areas such as Mount Yoshino, near Kyoto, attract millions of sight-seers to groves filled with the beautiful blossoming trees. The following Japanese folk song, "Sakura," typifies the poetry about Japan's beloved flower:

Sakura, sakura, yayoino sorawa,
Miwatasu kagiri; kasumika kumoka,
Nioi zo izuru; iza ya iza ya,
Miniyakan.

Sakura, sakura, now is cherry blossom time,
Clouds of petals fill the sky; perfume floats
   like mist in the air,
Blossoms fragrant everywhere; sakura,
   sakura,
Beauty in the springtime.

—*The Music Book: Grade 3.* 1984,
"Cherry Bloom," pp. 106-107.

Geography and Climate

Japan lies on an archipelago comprised of nearly 4,000 islands which form an arc along the eastern coast of Asia near China, Korea, and the Soviet Union. The majority of the population lives on the four largest islands: Hokkaido, Honshu, Shikoku, and Kyushu.

The archipelago stretches 2,000 miles, about the same as the distance from Maine to Florida. Its total land area, approximately 143,000 square miles, is approximately equal to California's and more than twice Wisconsin's. Overall, Japan is about one-twentieth the size of the United States.

Geography

While the geography of Japan is varied, the chain of volcanic mountains that divides Japan in two dominates the landscape. One side of the chain faces the Sea of Japan, and the other faces the Pacific Ocean. Many of the volcanoes remain active; however, the most famous peak, Mount Fuji (12,388 feet), has lain dormant for over 250 years.

The rivers are short and swift-flowing because of the mountainous topography and the narrow width of the land. Although most of the rivers are not navigable, they are important for industrial purposes, hydroelectricity, irrigation, and domestic water supplies.

About 29 percent of Japan's land consists of plains and basins. Whereas urban expansion invades much of this land, the flat river deltas are still used for irrigated rice fields.

Hundreds of peninsulas, bays, and small islands dot the coastline. Like California, Japan's coastal scenery provides great variety—from sandy beaches to rugged cliffs.

Like that of the United States' East Coast, Japan's weather varies considerably from north to south. Hokkaido's cold and snow in winter attracts skiers, while southern Kyushu offers sun and surf.

Weather

The sea surrounding Japan tempers the weather. During the winter a cold wind from eastern Siberia blows across the Sea of Japan, bringing frigid weather to the windward side of the two northern islands, Honshu and Hokkaido. Meanwhile, the Pacific side enjoys milder weather and low humidity. In the summer, wind from the Pacific Ocean brings warm temperatures and higher humidity. The rainy season, *tsuyu* (meaning plum rains), lasts from early June to mid-July and affects the entire country. These rains, primarily fine and misty, may annoy tourists and urbanites with perpetual dampness, but they delight farmers and gardeners. The rains occasionally bring torrential downpours that result in flooding or violent typhoons, especially in the southern parts of Kyushu. The typhoons, which hit in late summer and fall, often cause flooding, landslides, and property destruction, but are usually short-lived.

Geography and Climate

Japan

Area	145,834 square miles 377,765 square kilometers
Population	121,150,000 (1987 est.) Seventh largest population in the world
Density	321 persons per square kilometer (247.11 per acre)
Capital	Tokyo: population—26 million in metropolitan area 8.4 million in city of Tokyo
Climate	Similar to the eastern United States Variable from north to south, temperate to subtropically warm Patterns affected by landforms, ocean currents, monsoon winds, and alignment of the islands
Neighboring Countries	USSR (north), Korea (west), and China (southwest)
Official Language	Japanese
Ethnic Background	Probably descendants of people from all over Southeast Asia and the Pacific, but now merged into one distinctive group
Principal Religions	Shinto, Buddhism, Christianity
Commercial Products	Crude steel, machines, electronics, biotechnology, office automation, automobiles, electrical appliances, computers and telecommunications equipment, shipbuilding, textiles, and fashion design
Currency	Yen (1988 exchange rate: $1.00 U.S. = 130 yen)
Government	Constitutional monarchy with sovereignty resting with the people
Head of Government	Prime Minister

Geography and Climate

Wisconsin – Japan: A Comparison

	Wisconsin	Japan
Area	56,153 sq. miles	145,834 sq. miles
Distance	320 miles (north to south) (515 km)	1,200 miles (northeast to southwest) (1,900 km)
Highest Elevation	1,952 ft. Price County (595 meters)	12,388 ft. Mount Fuji (3,776 meters)
Population	4,705,642 (1980)	121,150,000 (1987 est.)
Largest City	Milwaukee 636,297 Metropolitan area 1,397,143	Tokyo 8,349,209 Metropolitan area 11,615,069
Density of Population	84 persons per sq. mile (32 persons per sq. km)	831 persons per sq. mile (321 persons per sq. km)
Distribution of Population	64% urban 36% rural	77% urban 23% rural
Average Temperature	Milwaukee High Low January 29°F 15°F July 81° 61°	Tokyo High Low January 46°F 30°F July 81° 61°
Location	Madison 43°N, 89°W Beloit 42°N, 89°W Superior 46.4°N, 92°W	Tokyo 35.4°N, 139.4°E Nagasaki 32.4°N, 129.5°E Sapporo 43°N, 141°E

Geography and Climate

Japanese Population Density (1985)

Population per Square Kilometer

- 1000 and over
- 500 and 999
- 300 and 499
- 200 and 299
- under 199 persons

Geography and Climate

Population Density by Country (1984)

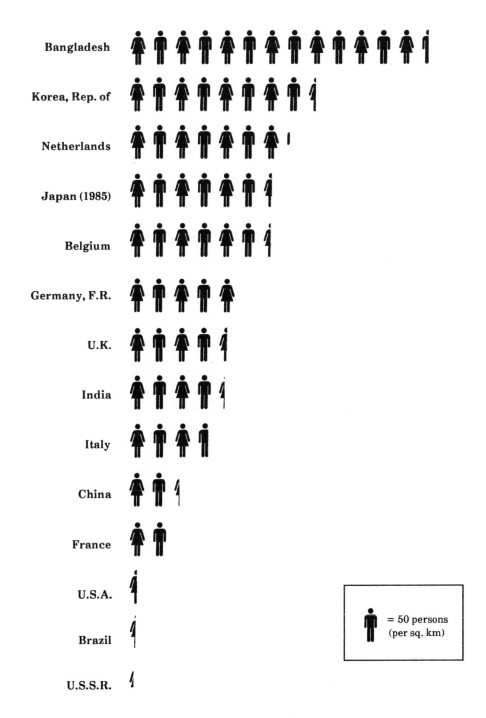

Bangladesh	
Korea, Rep. of	
Netherlands	
Japan (1985)	
Belgium	
Germany, F.R.	
U.K.	
India	
Italy	
China	
France	
U.S.A.	
Brazil	
U.S.S.R.	

= 50 persons
(per sq. km)

Activities: History and Geography

2

History—Then and Now

Activity 1: Elementary Level

These are sample activities, or examplars, only. They can be used as described or re-modeled to suit local needs. They also may suggest ideas for additional history experiences for elementary students.

Objectives

● To discover how and when Japanese and American communities began
● To compare the early occupations of Japanese and American communities
● To find out what contributions were made by Japanese and American communities a long time ago and compare them with contemporary contributions of the countries
● To reinforce basic reference skills, such as using an index and alphabetical ordering

Materials

● Compton's *Precyclopedia, World Book Encyclopedia, Lands and People* (Grolier), other general reference materials, trade books on Japan, an anthology of folk tales from Japan and North America, including American Indian tales, and *National Geographic* or tourism magazines
● Construction paper, felt markers, scissors, pencils, modeling clay, pictures, glue, Japanese items from home
● Activity Sheet 1: Comparison of Communities and 3: My Tale of Early Japan
● Specific titles that might be helpful including
   —"Nobles and Samurai," *Video Letter from Japan*
   —*We the People: The Story of the U.S. Constitution* by Peter Spier. Doubleday, 1987.
   —*Frontier Living* and *Colonial Living* by Edwin Tunis. Both Crowell, 1976.

Suggested Procedures

1. Using Activity Sheet 1: Comparison of Communities, children will work on a short research project assigned by the teacher. After research is completed, groups may share information and record it on a large chart for class discussion. Suggested cities to look up might include:

Japan	U.S.	Wisconsin
Nagasaki	Miami, Florida	Milwaukee
Osaka	Santa Fe, New Mexico	Green Bay
Hiroshima	Boston, Massachusetts	Eau Claire
Sapporo	New Orleans, Louisiana	Student's community

2. Individuals or partners will browse through or read Japanese and American folk tales, looking for occupations of the characters. In Japanese tales they should easily find jobs like woodcutter, fisherman, priest, homemaker, princess, or warrior. On a bulletin board have students display symbols of the occupations they've found, citing the stories from which they came. The bulletin board display can be used as a reading-challenge device or a guessing game of the occupations.

3. Have students use their imaginations as well as their research skills to develop a museum of Japanese and American artifacts. Individuals or partners can collect items that reflect the life of Japanese and American communities of long ago and today. Items might include equipment needed for a tea ceremony, formed out of clay; a kimono on a doll; a bowl of rice to symbolize rural communities. Edwin Tunis' books provide numerous ideas for contributions of early Americans, such as weaving, farming, and blacksmithing. Peter Spier's book will be helpful for understanding early Americans' contributions to government and the U.S. Constitution. Native American contributions might include corn, planting techniques, democratic government, birchbark canoes, housing, and healing remedies. Contributions of contemporary Japan and America can be shown by a collage or scrap book showing pictures of products.

Follow-Up Activity

Have students draw upon their newfound information to write a short tale about life in early Japan, using Activity Sheet 3: My Tale of Early Japan. These stories might be compiled in a booklet and added to the classroom library or the school's instructional media center.

Additional Easy Activity

Make a large mural exhibiting a particular historic moment, for example, the arrival of Commodore Perry in 1853, the Winter Olympics in Sapporo in 1976, or the cultural contributions of Toyotomi Hideyoshi in the sixteenth century (the tea ceremony, architecture, the theater). Display the mural in the library of hallway, adding information labels so that other students can read about Japan.

History—Then and Now

Comparison of Communities

Japan		
Community Name	**Date of Founding**	**Type of Community***

United States		
Community Name	**Date of Founding**	**Type of Community***

Wisconsin		
Community Name	**Date of Founding**	**Type of Community***

*Type of community means rural or urban, what kinds of businesses or industries are located there, what people did there a long time ago, what they do today. You may find other interesting things to note about this community.

History—Then and Now

Questions for Discussion

. Who settled the communities?

. How old are the communities?

. What was it like to live a long time ago?

. What did people do a long time ago and how do those occupations compare with those of today?

. In which ways have these people contributed to the rest of the world?

. What buildings or events reflect pride in the community's history and traditions?

History—Then and Now

My Tale of Early Japan

A long time ago in the _____ of _____
town/village

a _____ named _____ was sitting near
man/woman

the _____. _____ was wearing _____
He/She

_____. _____ was feeling very
He/She

_____ for that day was _____

_____. _____ was thinking hard because
He/She

_____ didn't know what to do about _____
he/she

_____.

It was a difficult problem—but along came a _____

and this is how the problem was solved: _____

_____

_____

_____

_____

_____

20

Japan: History, Land, and Climate

Activity 2: Elementary/Intermediate Level

This activity was contributed by Charlotte Myhers, a fourth-grade teacher and unit leader in the Osseo-Fairchild School District, Osseo, Wisconsin.

These are sample activities, or examplars, only. They can be used as described or re-modeled to suit local needs. They also may suggest ideas for additional history, land, and climate experiences for elementary and intermediate level students.

Objectives

- To compare Japan's historical form of government with that of contemporary Japan
- To investigate Japan's geographical features in an atlas or on a map
- To compare the climate and the sizes of Japan and Wisconsin
- To review information through use of a crossword puzzle

Materials

- Activity Sheet 1: Japan's history, land, and climate
- World atlas
- Activity sheets 2 and 3: maps of Japan, Wisconsin, and the United States
- A world almanac
- Activity Sheet 4: Crossword Puzzle

Suggested Procedures

1. Discuss Japan's geographical features with students.
2. Each student will read the background information and investigate research questions on Activity Sheet 1.
3. Through group discussion, the teacher can help students compare Japan and Wisconsin, using information they have gathered.
4. For further review, have students complete the crossword puzzle, Activity Sheet 4.

Additional Easy Activities

1. Make large wall maps outlining Japan and Wisconsin. Using library references such as *Land and Peoples* and the *National Geographic World Atlas*, locate major cities and significant sites such as Mt. Fuji. Using colored stick-on dots, mark the sites and label them or make a key to the colored labels. With large pins and paper banners, locate some of the major sites that tourists might visit in Wisconsin and Japan.
2. Design a climate and time zone chart to show comparisons between Wisconsin and Japan. Paper plates with movable hands will show the contrasts in time zones. Movable ribbons in slots on cardboard thermometers may be used to show average seasonal weather differences. Make two sets of thermometers, one to show Fahrenheit, the other Celsius measurements.

Japan: History, Land, and Climate

History

The history of a country is an account of the important events that have happened over many years. Histories are usually written beginning with the oldest events and ending with the most recent ones.

A long time ago, before it became a modern industrial country, Japan was divided into small farms and villages. There were no large cities like Tokyo or Osaka.

In each part of the country, a group of farms was ruled by a *daimyo* or lord. Each daimyo built a castle to protect himself and his land against other daimyos. The castle was built in the middle of farms that were controlled by the daimyo. In return for his protection against bandits and other intruders, the farmers paid the lord with rice and vegetables. The daimyo paid fierce samurai—knights or warriors—to help him protect his family and the farmers.

The strongest daimyo in Japan made himself emperor or ruler of all the other daimyos in the country.

This method of governing a country, with emperor, daimyo, samurai, and farmers, closely resembled the feudal system in Europe during the Middle Ages.

There is still an emperor in Japan today, even though Japan is a democratic country with representatives elected by the people. The emperor is a symbolic head of the country and does not make or enforce the laws. The emperor's position is similar to that of the Queen of England.

Land

Japan is made up of four large islands plus many small ones. The four largest ones are called Honshu, Kyushu, Shikoku, and Hokkaido. Consult your maps. Tokyo is the largest city. Which island is it on? On which island is Sapporo located? Locate the oceans and sea that surround Japan. Why is one called an "ocean" and the other a "sea"?

At one time Mount Fuji was a very active volcano. The last time it erupted was 1707. Today it is a popular vacation area and almost 500,000 people climb it yearly. Locate Mount Fuji on the map. Which island is it on? What else can you learn about this famous mountain?

Japan is 3,000 kilometers long. How does this compare with the distance between Beloit and Ashland? How does it compare with the distance from Texas to Wisconsin?

Climate

The climate is not the same all over Japan. Hokkaido is cold and snowy in winter, making it a good place for skiers. Honshu Island has a mild winter, but snow falls on Mount Fuji near Tokyo.

Source: Adapted from the series *The Countries and Festivals of the World,* Crabtree Publications, 1977.

Tokyo's average temperatures are:

January	3.7° C	(38.6° F)
February	13.1° C	(55.5° F)
July	25.1° C	(77° F)
October	16.7° C	(62° F)

Which island has the warmest climate? Compare these temperatures with the average seasonal temperatures where you live.

Japan: History, Land and Climate

Comparative Sizes of Japan and Wisconsin

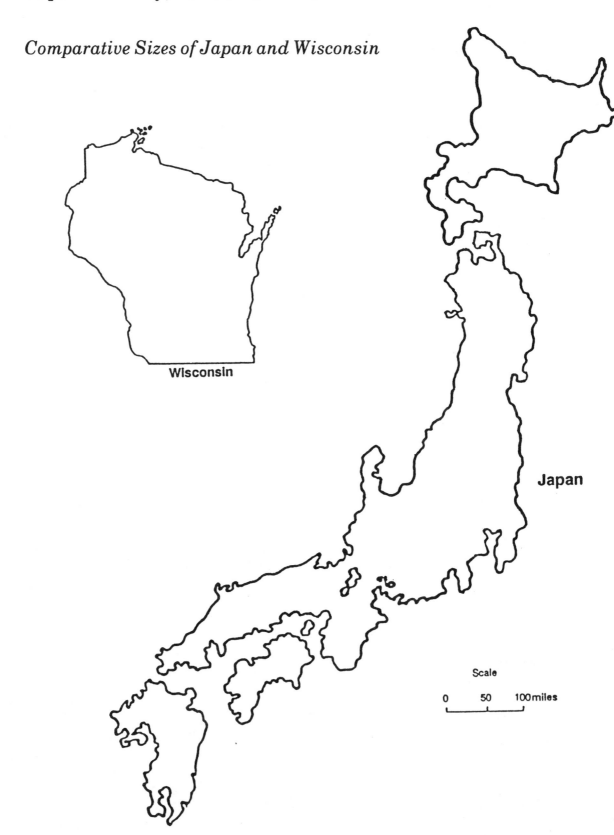

Wisconsin

Japan

Scale

0   50   100 miles

Japan: History, Land and Climate

Comparative Sizes of Japan and U.S.

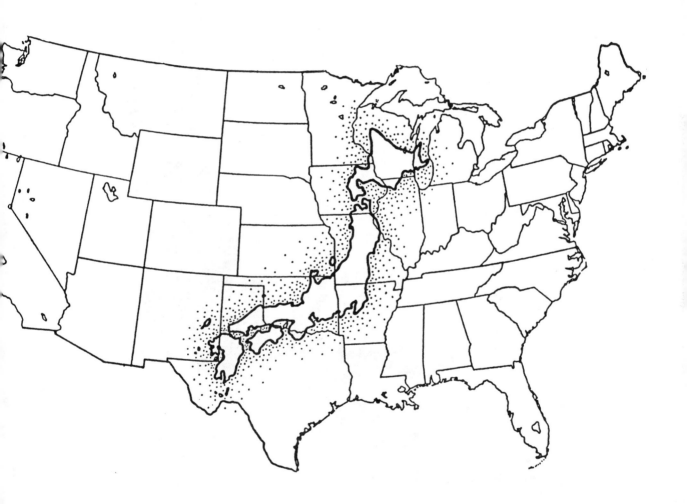

Japan: History, Land and Climate

Crossword Puzzle

Complete this crossword puzzle using information you have learned.
Some words may appear more than once.

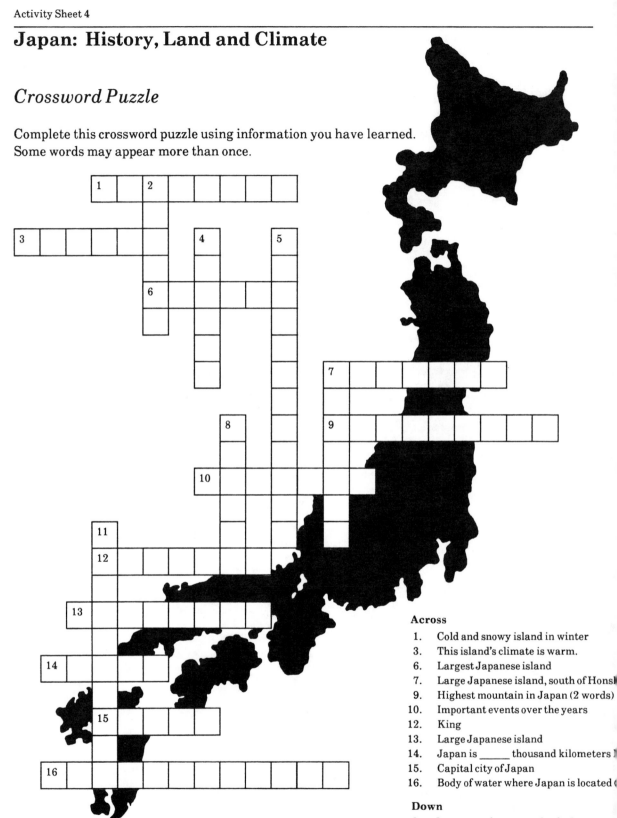

Across

1. Cold and snowy island in winter
3. This island's climate is warm.
6. Largest Japanese island
7. Large Japanese island, south of Hons
9. Highest mountain in Japan (2 words)
10. Important events over the years
12. King
13. Large Japanese island
14. Japan is _____ thousand kilometers
15. Capital city of Japan
16. Body of water where Japan is located

Down

2. Largest and most southerly Japanese
4. Mild climate
5. Government during the Middle Ages
7. Fierce knights of ancient Japan
8. Ruler or lord of ancient Japan
11. Today, Japan is a _____ country.

Solution appears on page 179.

Major Changes When East Meets West

Activity 3: Intermediate Level

These are sample activities, or examplars, only. They can be used as described or re-modeled to suit local needs. They also may suggest ideas for additional cultural experiences for intermediate level students.

Objectives

● To analyze cultural changes that occurred in Japan as a result of Commander Perry's arrival in 1853 and the bombing of Hiroshima and Nagasaki in 1945
● To predict how the relationship between Japan and the United States might change in the future

Materials

● General reference books and trade books about the history of nineteenth- and twentieth-century Japan.
● Articles from recent periodicals and newspapers about Japan-U.S. relations
● "Japan: Technology and Tradition" filmstrips
● *Commodore Perry and the Shogun,* by Rhonda Blumberg (multiple copies needed), and Activity Sheet 1.
● *A Place Called Hiroshima,* by Betty Lipton (multiple copies needed), and Activity Sheet 2.
● *Hiroshima No Pika,* by Toshi Maruki
● Activity Sheet 3: Questions for Discussion

Suggested Procedures

1. Ask half the class to read Blumberg and the other half to read Lipton and skim Maruki. The entire class should read current periodicals and newspapers. (It would be helpful to have students supply articles about U.S.-Japanese affairs.)
2. Have students use activity sheets 1 and 2 as their reading guides.
3. Organize small-group discussions to focus on the study questions and the articles from current periodicals and newspapers.
4. Alternate filmstrip viewing with the small-group discussion periods.

Follow-Up Activities

Nineteenth-Century Group
1. Students may compose short scripts based on scenes from Blumberg's book. One idea might be to dramatize and act out the reception given to the Japanese on the "Powhatan," Perry's ship; another might focus on the reaction of the people in Shimoda when the Americans came to visit.

2. Suggest students write a newspaper article that might have appeared in a Japanese newspaper when Perry was finally allowed to come ashore. Comparing details of the Americans' clothing, manners, and conversations should help explain the shock the Japanese felt.
3. Encourage students to write a letter from Commodore Perry to his home, describing his reactions and the events that occurred as the American fleet waited for permission to land. A description of the gift exchanges, the messages, the courtesy tactics, and the unusual personalities encountered will add interest.

Twentieth-Century Group
1. Plan and present a short discussion about world peace, using arguments based on the events of Hiroshima and Nagasaki. Participants may portray world leaders, such as secretaries of state or prime ministers; another group might wish to portray citizens, or they may wish to portray themselves: school students who are concerned about the future.
2. Ask students to write a diary as if they were returning to Japan for the first time, in 1946, after 20 years of living in Canada. Search for family, friends, and familiar places.
3. Tell students they are assigned to an "advance team" for a television network that will produce a documentary on changes in Japan from 1945 to 1988. They must plan a sequence that concentrates on the changes from a military government to a democracy, from devastation to rebirth, from the old society to a modern one. Students should outline places to see, interviews of interest, family life, and so on. They also should write a short introduction and conclusion for the documentary.

Additional Easy Activity

After reading *Sadako and the Thousand Paper Cranes* by Eleanor Coerr, construct a peace monument and learn about the efforts to honor Sadako through Peace Day (August 6) in Japan. Discuss ideas the students in the school might use to develop a local peace celebration, then plan for that event. Invite a local politician to join in your celebration.

Major Changes When East Meets West

Questions for Discussion

Discuss these questions, using information you have gained from reading *Commodore Perry and the Shogun*, by Rhonda Blumberg.

1. What factors encouraged Perry to embark on this mission?

2. List some of the "game" tactics used by both the Americans and the Japanese during the first contacts.

3. Predict what might have happened if the Americans had not been allowed to enter Japan.

4. What changes occurred in Japan as a result of Perry's expedition?

5. Why is an isolationist policy difficult for any nation to maintain in the modern world?

Major Changes When East Meets West

Questions for Discussion

Discuss these questions, using information you have gained from reading *A Place Called Hiroshima*, by Betty Lipton.

1. What were the immediate effects of the bombing of Hiroshima?

2. What were the long-term effects on the health of people, the economy, urbanization, family life, and culture?

3. How do you suppose the bombing of Hiroshima affects the attitudes of Japanese as they look toward the future?

4. In your opinion, what is the significance of Lipton's book?

Major Changes When East Meets West

Questions for Discussion

1. What factors shape cultures?

2. How can people understand one another when they don't speak the same langauge?

3. In what ways are cultural regions of the world changing today?

4. How can conflicts between nations be resolved and how can we promote peace?

5. How is the future of the United States tied to the future of the world?

Culture 3

Homes, Food, and Clothing

Homes

The architecture of Japanese houses reflects the country's environment. The climate is damp during the rainy season and often hot during the summer. Houses are typically designed for maximum ventilation. Most interior rooms have at least one or two walls that consist of sliding doors called *fusuma*. These doors, together with wide sliding doors on the outside walls, can be opened wide to let in the cool air. In winter they can be closed to prevent drafts.

Weather Adaptations

Because the winter is mild in most parts of the country, except in the north, houses often do not have central heating. Instead, rooms used for daily living are located in the center of the house and are surrounded by long corridors which offer protection and insulation from the weather. In winter only rooms in use are heated, usually by small gas or kerosene heaters called *sutohbu*, a term adapted from the English word "stove."

In winter, Japanese also often sit around a *kotatsu*, a wooden frame containing an electric heater over which a quilt or blanket is thrown. These kotatsu are usually about the same size as a table, except that the legs are short. They are an excellent way to keep feet and legs warm. On a cold winter evening, many families will gather around the kotatsu and perhaps watch television or simply share each other's company. The kotatsu thus serves the same social function as a fireplace in an American home. Largely because of the frugal use of energy for heating, homes in Japan consume only about one-quarter as much energy as do American homes.

Size and Arrangements

Japanese houses are generally much smaller than American houses due to the scarcity of land. Japanese homes have about the same amount of floor space (80 square meters) as homes in France or West Germany—countries which, like Japan, are rather densely populated. As might be expected, homes in rural areas tend to be larger and have more adjoining land than homes in urban areas.

Japanese rooms do not have much furniture and are often used for several purposes: sleeping, eating, living, and playing. To conserve space, Japanese sleep on futons, or folding mattresses, which are spread out on the floor at night and stored away in closets during the day. Except for the kitchen and perhaps a carpeted living room, floors are covered with *tatami*, or rice straw mats, which are comfortable to sit on and provide insulation in the winter.

Usually, one room in a house will have a *tokonoma*, or small alcove, where flower arrangements are displayed and scroll paintings are hung. There is also usually a small shelf containing a miniature Shinto shrine and a Buddhist altar where offerings are made to ancestral spirits.

Construction and Conveniences

Before World War II, almost all buildings in Japan were made of wood with either a straw or tile roof. Most buildings were only one or two stories high because of the constant danger of earthquakes. In recent years, however, as lumber has risen in price, Japanese have begun using concrete, aluminum, and other modern building materials. Many homes today are of prefabricated construction. New advances in earthquake-proof building technology have also made possible skyscrapers of 60 stories and more which are radically changing the skylines of Japanese cities.

All Japanese homes today have electricity and running water, and most have flush toilets. About 60 percent of all Japanese families live in houses they own, while about 30 percent live in rented houses or apartments. The remainder live in public housing or in company-provided housing.

To most Americans, Japanese homes might seem small and cramped, but after one has lived in Japan for a period of time and adjusted to Japanese lifestyles these homes lose their sense of "smallness." Conversely, when Japanese arrive in the United States, they can feel lost in the spacious scale of some American homes.

The design of Japanese homes is well adapted to the needs of Japanese society. Their compact scale helps reinforce the closely knit structure of the Japanese family. Family members live closely together and must regulate their behavior to avoid conflicts. Outside the home, Japanese like to feel a sense of belonging to groups (such as classmates or coworkers). Japanese society places considerable importance on striving for harmony and cooperation in human relations.

Food

Most Americans have eaten at Japanese restaurants and are familiar with some traditional Japanese foods, the custom of eating at low tables, and the use of *ohashi*, or chopsticks, as utensils. When they travel to Japan they may be surprised to find *Makudonarudo*, or McDonald's, with the same golden arches, burgers, fries, and shakes as are familiar in America. This is a popular spot in Japan just as it is in Wisconsin. Kentucky Fried Chicken, Shakey's Pizza, Mister Donut, and Dairy Queen also have franchises in Japan.

Traditional Meals

In Japanese homes and restaurants one can find many foods that are not found on the dinner tables of most Wisconsin families. Just as dairy and meat products often form the nucleus of meals in this state of dairy farms, Japanese eating habits have been formed by their geography and environment. Algae or *kaiso*, a sea vegetable rich in iodine, is an important part of the diet. Its many species have sustained people in times of starvation, protected against diseases, prevented hardening of the arteries, and helped produce healthy complexions. *Tofu*, or soybean curd, dates back more than 2,000 years to China, and was later used by Buddhist monks forbidden, until 1869, to eat meat. Used as a main ingredient and meat substitute, it provides protein and bulk. Other favorite soybean products are *shoyu* (soy sauce) and *miso*, a fermented bean paste.

The traditional Japanese diet is not based on high cholesterol foods, and it is only in recent years, with the advent of American fast food franchises and imported beef, that eating habits have begun to change. Only 16 percent of the country is suitable for cultivation, but the country has liberal access to the ocean's bounty. Therefore fish long has been a staple food; it is served either cooked or raw. Much of the existing arable land is used to produce rice. This is served as the main course of most meals, often topped with sliced pork or chicken, beef, eel, or eggs. Sushi shops, found all over Japan, specialize in packed rice dishes, sometimes served with toppings such as marinated or boiled fish.

The serving of a Japanese meal is considered an art. The natural appearance of the food is important to preserve, so it is arranged on separate plates or dishes to emphasize harmony of shape, size, and color. The use of fresh foods, in season shows the Japanese appreciation of nature. Fresh vegetables or fruits may be cut in a way that suggests a bird, flower, or leaf depending on the season and occasion. Containers of pottery, lacquerware, porcelain, or bamboo are carefully selected to contribute to the serving of the cuisine. The setting of the meal also is considered in an attempt to emphasize serenity and harmony. Foods are cut into bite-sized pieces before serving, so there is no need for knives and forks.

Fast Food

Not all meals are eaten in the relaxed atmosphere of the home or restaurant. There are convenient substitutes for the busy commuter or harried student. Street vendors, *yatai-mise*, specialize in hot foods like barbecued chicken or baked sweet potatoes. *Sunakkubaa* are coffee and sake bars that stay open all night providing snacks and music, along with liquid refreshments. *Ekiben* or *bento* are box lunches available at train stations. They contain cold foods unique to the geographical location in a variety almost like a Scandinavian smorgasbord's. Typical ingredients might include meat, fish, vegetables, eggs, pickles, and perhaps a field of white rice with a sour red plum in the center to represent the Japanese flag. It is said that there are at least 1,600 varieties of bento!

Clothing

The dress code for young people is similar, whether in Tokyo or Madison: blue jeans, tennis shoes, and T-shirts, especially those printed with college names or clever slogans, are popular. All over Japan one sees fashions resembling those worn in Eau Claire, Milwaukee, or La Crosse.

Most children must wear uniforms for school—usually navy blue or black skirts for girls, slacks with white shirts for boys. Workers are usually dressed in uniforms, reinforcing the idea of pride in their company and a sense of camaraderie among the wearers.

The Kimono

Although most people wear western-style clothes for their everyday affairs, the traditional and best-known garment, the kimono, is still considered the national dress. An import to Japan, it was brought from China by Buddhist monks in the eighth century. It is still worn today by some older women and by teachers of classes, such as flower arranging, but its primary use is for special festivals and ceremonies.

The kimono is a wrap-around robe with long, dangling sleeves. A sash or *obi* is wrapped around the waist to hold the robe closed. Traditionally, the garment was made of linen, silk, or cotton, but now kimonos are also available in synthetic fabrics, making them less expensive.

Although the style has remained virtually unchanged since early times, the colors and patterns make each kimono unique. Selection depends on the age of the wearer, the occasion, or the season of the year. Young, unmarried women wear the most brightly colored kimonos. More subdued colors are favored by married and mature women. For formal occasions, such as weddings or funerals, kimonos might be black or white; some are decorated with the family crest.

At one time young girls studied the art of kimono-making as part of their schooling. Although today's curriculum doesn't include this course, there are evening courses available in the sewing and wearing of kimonos.

Men also wear kimonos, mainly at home. They might also wear a skirt-like garment, called a *hakama*, and a loose upper garment, *montsuki*, on formal occasions.

A light kimono, *yukata*, is worn at home on hot summer evenings, especially after a relaxing bath. But on cold winter nights, a cozy flannel *nemaki* feels good, particularly where central heating is not available.

Shoes and Slippers

Americans are aware of the Japanese tradition of removing their shoes when entering a home. For Wisconsinites, accustomed to wearing boots most of the winter, changing footwear is a familiar habit. Inside a traditional Japanese home the *surippa* (slippers) are changed at certain room borders. For example, one would not wear house slippers into the bathroom; special plastic slippers are worn there. When entering a room where the floor is covered with *tatami* mats, the slippers are left at the threshold.

For outdoor use the traditional Japanese shoe, the *geta*, is used. This is a flat wooden platform on two thin lateral stilts with a thong for the foot, originally designed for use on muddy streets. The getas are worn with stockings designed with a separate toe area—like the thumb of a mitten—to accommodate the thonged shoe. For summer use, getas are cool and convenient, but for fast walking and more formal occasions, most Japanese prefer western-style shoes.

Writing and Language

Writing Systems

The Japanese written language is highly complex. It is composed of three different systems. Two of them, called *hiragana* and *katakana*, are roughly equivalent to the English alphabet. Each consists of forty-eight symbols, and each symbol represents a sound, typically composed of a consonant and a vowel. For example, *ka* can be written か or カ depending on which system is used. These syllables are combined to form words. Hiragana is used to "spell out" Japanese words, conjugate verbs, and perform other syntactical functions. Katakana is used to write words borrowed from foreign languages, as in *besuboru* (baseball).

The third symbol system, *kanji*, adapted from the Chinese, is unlike anything in English. In this system each symbol or character conveys an idea; each character may have several pronunciations, the proper one being determined by context. There are over 7,000 characters in a commonly used dictionary; 1,900 of them are considered basic for literacy, and everyone must learn to read and write them before leaving school.

All three systems are used simultaneously in written Japanese. Take for example, the sentence, "I want to go to America.": 私は　アメリカへ　行きたい 。

The underlined kanji mean "I" and "go." The word "America" is written in katakana, and the other symbols are all hiragana, indicating grammatical functions and the desire "to go."

Japanese, like English, has incorporated many words from other languages. Chinese words that have recently been added to the Japanese vocabulary include: *kare raisu* (curry rice), *suto* (strike), and *infure* (inflation). These words have been both shortened and Japanized.

A number of English words have been creatively adapted by the Japanese to form words or meanings not found in English. Examples are *naitah* (nighter), a baseball game played at night, and *ruzu* (loose), meaning slovenly or slipshod.

Words of Japanese origin used in the United States include: shogun, samurai, sukiyaki, sake, kimono, and tsunami. An example of a word that has changed its meaning is hibachi, which in Japan refers to a large porcelain pot partially filled with charcoal and used for warmth—not for a barbecue.

In the intermediate grades, Japanese students begin learning to read the Roman alphabet used in writing English. Although still unfamiliar to and not used by many older Japanese, it frequently appears in advertising.

Writing and Language

Japanese and English Words and Phrases

Pronunciation guide

Vowels in Japanese are pronounced like those in Romance languages and are more similar to Italian than to English.

A   as in "ah!"

E   as in "pen" or "dent"

I   as in "inn" (when it appears in the middle of a word)

I   as in "see" (when it appears at the end of a word)

O   as in "oh" or "no"

U   as in "mood"

U   as in "hood"

Most consonants are pronounced as they are in English. Double consonants should have twice the emphasis as single ones (kon-nichi wa). As in English, some sounds are dropped or said less emphatically. A few consonants are separated from vowels by a "y" as in "Tokyo." These are slightly stressed, making "kyo" sound almost like one syllable.

The following diphthongs are pronounced as follows:

samurai   as in "kaiser"

geisha   as in "reindeer"

Getting acquainted

Good day	Konnichi-wa
Hello	Hello or Haro
Good-bye	Sayonara
Good evening	Konban wa
Good night	Oyasumi nasai
Good health	O genki de
See you soon	Mata ne (or Ja mata)
What is your name?	Onamae wa?
My name is _____.	Watakushi wa _____ desu.

Politeness

Thanks	Domo
Thank you	Domo arigato
Thank you very much	Domo arigato gozaimasu
Excuse me.	Sumimasen.
That's too bad.	Zannen desu.

Useful phrases

I understand.	Wakarimasu.
I don't understand.	Wakarimasen.
Do you understand?	Wakarimasu ka?
How do you say it in Japanese?	Nihongo dewa nan to iimasu-ka?
Do you speak English?	Anata wa eigo o hanashimasu-ka?
(Speak) slowly please.	Yukkuri (iite) kudasai.
How much is it?	Ikura desu ka?

Numbers (Chinese system)

1	ichi	6	roku
2	ni	7	shichi (or nana)
3	san	8	hachi
4	shi (or yon)	9	ku (or kyu)
5	go	10	ju

Days of the week

Sunday	Nichi-yobi
Monday	Getsu-yobi
Tuesday	Ka-yobi
Wednesday	Sui-yobi
Thursday	Moku-yobi
Friday	Kin-yobi
Saturday	Do-yobi

Seasons

Spring	Haru
Summer	Natsu
Autumn	Aki
Winter	Fuyu

Directions

North	Kita
South	Minami
East	Higashi
West	Nishi

Basic Vocabulary

address	jusho	little	chiisai
bank	ginko	man	otoko no hito
bad	warui	map	chizu
beautiful	utsu kushii	money	okane
big	ookii	morning	asa
book	hon	newspaper	shinbun
boy	otoko no ko	night	yoru
building	biru	no	iie
bus	basu	right (direction)	migi
castle	shiro	river	kawa
cheap	yashui	road	michi (or dori)
chopsticks	hashi	school	gakko
cold (chilly)	kaze	sick	byooki
difficult	muzukashii	street	tori
drink	nomu	student	gakusei
eat	taberu	teacher	sensei
exit	deguchi	this	kono
expensive	takai	that	sono
far	toi	today	kyo
flower	hana	tomorrow	ashita
girl	onna-no-ko	toilet	toire (or toiretto)
good	ii (or yoi)	water	mizu
here	koko	when?	itsu?
hot	atsui	where?	doko?
I	Watashi wa	woman	onna no hito
left (direction)	hidari	yes	hai

Drama, Poetry, and Literature

Drama

Drama is one of Japan's most popular art forms. It is said that *noh*, the oldest form of Japanese drama, began much earlier than the fourteenth century, but it was during the period of samurai patronage that it began to flourish. It traces its origins to the dances and songs offered at Buddhist shrines. In these stylized dance performances, all characters (male and female) are portrayed by men who wear elaborate costumes and masks. The movement is slow, and the symbolism complex. Musical accompaniment is provided by a shrill flute and the rhythmic beats of three drums. The 250 noh plays are grouped into five categories: God, man, woman, madness, and demons.

Kyogen

Kyogen is a form of comic drama representing the everyday lives of common people—their quarrels, funny expressions, attempts to outwit one another, daydreams, and fantasies. Although the plays are over 600 years old, their messages are timeless and universal. In contrast with noh drama, there are no masks, and the costumes are subdued; the play's plot is revealed primarily through dialogue and spatial relationships rather than through dance. These lively plays were originally performed during the intermission of noh performances.

Kabuki

The romantic *Kabuki* plays are the most recognized and enjoyable form of Japanese drama for Westerners. A simplified definition of Kabuki is "to dance and sing," derived from *ka* (dance) and *bu* (sing). Originally these plays were performed by women who imitated men, but as the performances became more bawdy, women players were banned and the roles given only to men.

Today, these rather melodramatic plays are still elaborately staged with frequent costume changes, the use of masks, and much action. The staging is often done with revolving sets that can be changed quickly, and also with the aid of black-clad assistants who move about on stage during the play without distracting the audience. Western visitors are usually surprised at the casual atmosphere of the Kabuki theater where audience participation is the norm, with people coming and going, and interruptions including eating and drinking. As with noh and kyogen drama, however, Kabuki plays are highly stylized and are performed in much the same manner as they were in the 1700s, when they were at the height of their popularity.

Bunraku

The *Bunraku* is a form of drama in which the characters are played by nearly life-sized puppets. This form of drama originated in the sixteenth century but became popular through the playwright Chikamatsu Monzaemon in the seventeenth and early eighteenth centuries. Many of the plays depict famous love stories or stories of historical interest and have been used as plots for the kabuki dramas as well.

In Bunraku, the elaborately dressed and lifelike puppets are manipulated by three puppeteers dressed in black. One controls the head and right hand, one manipulates the left hand, and another, the feet. Bunraku puppets act out stories narrated in chants called *joururi*. The musical accompaniment is on a three-stringed instrument called a *shamisen*.

Poetry

Writing poetry in Japan is popular not only in the classroom or among professional writers, but also among the general population. At an international gathering of heads of state, Prime Minister Nakasone read haiku that he had written. Hundreds of haiku societies meet regularly, some with membership of more than 100 people. There are 600 magazines of haiku poetry published, many on a monthly basis, further attesting to the popularity of this form of expression.

Haiku

Haiku is a poetry form developed in the late seventeenth century by the poet Matsuo Basho. It was not until the late nineteenth century that this poetry took the name haiku. Basho had a deep reverence for nature, and this is why haiku poems are expressions about the seasons, flowers or other plant life, mountains, the sea, or the countryside.

The form of haiku is prescribed by tradition: a total of 17 syllables arranged in three lines of five, seven, and five syllables each. The third line expresses the solution or comments on what has been written in the first two. The last line is said to point to the heart of the idea. No words should be wasted, just as no unnecessary brush strokes should be added to a painting. To read and appreciate haiku, according to purists, one must re-create the poet's feeling in oneself and become a poet. Below are two examples of haiku. Translated into English, neither follows the 5-7-5 form of the original, but you can get a sense of the spirit of haiku from them.

> The sounds of scouring
> A saucepan blends
> With the tree-frog's voice.
> —Ryokan

> This autumn
> Why am I aging so?
> A bird flies toward the clouds.
> —Basho

Tanka

Tanka, another form of poetry, is an extension of haiku, enabling the poet to express emotion in more than 17 syllables. Tanka is much older than haiku and was included in the first Japanese poetry anthology, the *Manyoshu*, in the eighth century. It consists of 31 syllables and follows a 5-7-5-7-7 syllable pattern. The measure of success in a tanka poem is how powerfully the poet expresses the yearning for beauty, a feeling referred to as *yoyo*.

Literature

Japan's recorded literary history began in the eighth century A.D. Before that time, it is supposed, stories were transmitted orally. A few writings were attempted by the privileged class when writing was first introduced from China. Both the early oral expression and the first written literature arose from religious occasions and experiences. Narrative poems, songs, and histories were collected in the *Kojiki* (Record of Ancient Matters) and *Nihon Shoki* (Chronicles of Japan), the two earliest histories of Japan. These works allow modern students to learn something of those times, but are said to be full of distortions since the writers were still learning to work with the new and very difficult written language.

Novels

Japan's first novel was also the first known novel in the world—the famous *Genji Monogatari* or *Tale of Genji*. This literary monument, consisting of 54 volumes, was written in the early part of the eleventh century by a lady of the court, Murasaki Shikibu. *Tale of Genji* is a series of narratives about the lives, loves, intrigues, successes, and failures of the court nobles. This *monogatari*, or poetic narrative, provided the model for later fictional tales.

Another famous novel, *Heike Monogatari*, from the thirteenth century, won favorable and sympathetic audiences among warriors. This is the story of the Taira Clan's downfall in 1185. It reflects the interest in war tales typical of medieval times. The tale was memorized and told by storytellers as they traveled around the countryside.

Literature for the Common People

The content of Japanese literature changed during the sixteenth and seventeenth centuries. Comedies were abundant and contributed to the development of the puppet theater and the Kabuki drama. The written material of this period reflects more interest in common people's lives and character.

New literature flourished during the Tokagawa Era as well as an emphasis on traditional literary arts. Books that had been hand-printed could now be reproduced for wider availability. In addition, public education made literacy available to more people, including those who weren't part of the nobility. This period also marked the beginning of the lending library. Soon this enlarged readership became creators, as well as consumers, of literature.

Western Influence

The opening of Japan's doors to the western world brought additional influences to Japanese literature as English, French, and Russian books were translated into Japanese. Writers who helped provide the shift from the old Japanese literature to the new were Shimei Futabatei (1864-1909), Koyo Ozaki (1867-1903), and Roka Tokutomi (1868-1927). The first female writer since the eleventh and twelfth centuries was Akiko Yosano (1878-1942). Known for her *waka* poetry, she "offered a direct challenge to the constraints of feudalism and the old morality" through her writing.

In the early twentieth century, writers in Japan advocated social reform, but their efforts to bring more rapid change to Japan were met with censorship and suppression.

During World War II, literary freedom was completely suppressed, and many writers were imprisoned; since the early 1950s there has been a great resurgence of literary expression, making modern Japan one of the most dynamic contributors to world literature.

About 6,000 titles are published annually, and approximately 100 literary magazines are in publication; 30 literary awards are given annually in numerous fields. In 1968 Yasunari Kawabata won the Nobel Prize for Literature.

Arts, Traditions, and Festivals

Arts

Art in Japan is not limited to those who are especially talented. The widespread interest in art reflects the values of the educational system, as well as the fact that the Japanese feel very close to nature, everyday life, and religion.

Gardening and the tea ceremony, for instance, formalize ordinary matters of everyday life. Paper folding, or origami, is popular. A formal meal is artistically arranged by shape and color, presenting a feast for the eye, as well as the appetite. The spirit of the greatest paintings and literature is closely related to the spirit of Buddhism, which emphasizes harmony, serenity, and restraint. Buddhism also influences manners, dress, and home decor, which are both restrained and beautiful.

An interest in the arts is an important part of Japanese life, extending even into commercial enterprises. Large department stores reserve their top floors for art galleries and periodically exhibit paintings and sculpture from various eras. Workers and professional people attend art exhibits during their lunch hours. Popular interest in the arts also is reflected in many books, magazines, and newspapers.

Painting

The origin of Japan's painting can be traced to China. *Suiboku*, which were black and white line drawings, came to Japan along with Buddhism in the fifth and sixth centuries. As in the Western world, early painting was primarily influenced by religion, but later on literature was a strong influence on the development of secular art.

It was during the Edo Period (1603-1868) that one of the most popular forms of painting began. *Ukiyoe* (or *hanga*) paintings, which later became prints, were widely distributed and are thought to have been a strong influence on the French Impressionists. One form of woodblock printing, which used water colors with blocks cut from cherry wood, was developed by painters such as Utamaro, Harunobo, and Hiroshige.

Today's painting reflects the influence of Western art, but much of Japan's art retains the unique characteristics that have made it so universally appealing—harmony, serenity, and simplicity.

Handicrafts

Archaeologists and historians have learned about the early civilization of Wisconsin through fragments of pottery. Likewise, Japanese history has been partially revealed by the study of *jomon*, pieces of pottery from more than 9,000 years ago.

The development of the tea ceremony in the fifteenth century encouraged the development of ceramic art. At that time, Korean artisans were captured and hidden in secluded areas, where they produced beautiful works. Today one of the centers of this art is Arita, in northwest Kyushu; another is Mashiko, near Tokyo, where the master potter, Shoji Hamada, revived the traditional ceramic techniques earlier in this century.

Urushi, lacquerware, is another popular craft, and has found its way into import shops around the world. The wood of the *deigo* tree is used for the base of an article such as a bowl or box. After it is shaped, it is layered with varnish, painted with designs, then varnished again repeatedly until the surface is hard and shiny. Another style of lacquerware is *makie*, in which designs of gold, silver, or mother of pearl are embedded in the layers of varnish. Throughout Japanese history, urushi has been used for tables, tools, religious implements, and even to decorate weapons. The durability and usefulness of lacquerware is being challenged now by plastics, but the traditional artwork still is cherished by those who appreciate its craftsmanship.

Calligraphy

Calligraphy or *shodo*, the sister of painting in Japan, is a demanding and highly prized form of art. It was introduced by China, along with the *kanji* style of writing, and also was influenced by religious concepts. The key to success in shodo is the integration of mind and body in an expression of beauty.

Skill in calligraphy is not acquired overnight; rigorous training is demanded in brushwork techniques, composition, design, speed, and assertiveness. Shodo is drawn with a bamboo brush, using a dark India ink made from soot and glue. Different weights of paper or silk are used for calligraphy, and the completed scroll then is displayed in the *tokonoma*, a special area in the home reserved for showing art.

Traditionally, the art of calligraphy has been considered a mark of culture in Japan. It complemented poetry writing and still is used when special poems are written for the observance in early January called *Kakizome*, First Writing of the Year.

Flower Arranging

Ikebana, which means "living flowers," is more than the art of flower arrangement. Though the artist is creating a kind of sculpture, the object is more dynamic. Its composition is in the process of change, from bud to blossom and then to fading.

As in some of the other visual arts, there are specific rules for this re-creation of nature. Three main branches of the arrangement comprise its basic design: the tallest, *ten*, symbolizes heaven; the mid-branch, *jin*, represents man; the lowest is *chi*, or earth.

The art of ikebana is considered a basic skill for women. In earlier times, all young girls were required to study it before marriage. Today's working woman may take classes in this art, either for professional uses, such as interior decorating, or simply to enjoy the aesthetic value of ikebana.

Traditions

Japan's many elaborate and complex traditions are still an important part of Japanese life.

The Tea Ceremony

Chanoyu is a symbolic, ceremonial celebration of everyday tea and rice. Chanoyu involves more than simply drinking tea. It developed in the latter half of the fourteenth century out of the tea rituals of Zen temples. Two terms are associated with the tea ceremony: *cha-suki* (love of tea) and *cha yoriai* (tea gathering). The first term expresses the relationship between people and objects, and the second, the relationship between people.

As the tea ceremony developed, a reverence grew for Japanese utensils, both ceramic and simple, unadorned stoneware.

Traditionally, tea gatherings have included an element of amusement, as participants compete in trying to distinguish various kinds of tea. Those who can identify the regions where teas were grown receive prizes. Participants are expected to behave toward one another with wholehearted sincerity, as though the gathering were to be their only encounter in an entire lifetime. The object of chanoyu is to acquire serenity and peace of mind.

A complete tea ceremony lasts about four hours. First guests are served a light meal. Afterwards they often rest in the garden. Then the main ceremony begins, and the guests are served a thick, green tea. Later, they are served a lighter, foamy tea.

Formal Gardens

The art of landscape gardening, *niwa*, in Japan goes back to at least the sixth century. During the reign of the Empress-Regent Suiko (554-628), gardens with beautifully designed artificial hills and ornamental ponds were already popular.

The aim of Japanese landscape gardening is to create a miniature scenic landscape that suggests something on a large scale and looks completely natural.

Such gardens were an integral part of landscaping by the time Japan's imperial capital moved from Nagaokakyo to Kyoto in 794, where a garden of immense size, called *Shin Sen En* or Sacred Fountain Garden, was a centerpiece in the new city.

The introduction of Zen Buddhism into Japan during the Kamakura Period (1185-1336) had a significant influence on garden landscaping. Gardens became less decorative and were designed to impart a sense of tranquility and happiness.

The underlying philosophy of Japanese gardening is a combination of Shintoism, which reveres nature; Buddhism, which reveres life; and Zen, which seeks to perceive the fundamental reality in all things and abide by the laws of nature.

Generally speaking, there are three styles of Japanese gardens: the hill garden, which usually has a stream or pond in addition to several hills; the flat garden—used for meditation; and the tea garden, located next to the teahouse. Natural materials, such as shrubs, pebbles, sand, rock, trees, and water are used to symbolize woodlands, the sea, mountains, and waterfalls. A stone lantern might be added to represent a lighthouse, adding to the simple aesthetics of the garden.

The gardens of the palaces and temples, plus those of the feudal lords, still flourish in many areas of modern Japan, especially in Kyoto where more than 50 gardens are still open to the public.

Festivals

If schools in Japan were closed for every festival and holiday, children would rarely see the inside of a classroom! Japan's rich traditions flourish through an abundance of commemorations; there are celebrations occurring in some part of the country every day. Festivals honor the sea, mountains, flowers, the gods, the dead, children, grandparents, broken umbrellas, and even old hats.

The origin of many of the *matsuri* or festivals is religious and often agrarian, dating to the time when appeals were made to Buddhist and Shinto gods for a good planting season, favorable weather, and a bountiful harvest.

Major Celebrations

Ganjitsu, New Year's Day, January 1—This holiday time, also called *Oshogatsu*, is the most important time of celebration for Japanese as they welcome an opportunity to renew and to begin again. A wreath of pine, plum boughs, or bamboo is hung over the doorway to symbolize prosperity, purity, and longevity. A *shime-nawa*, a rope of straw and paper, is hung across the entryway to ward off evil spirits and to purify the home. Sweet sake, *toso*, is served along with a variety of foods, in hopes of good health in the new year.

Daruma Ichi, January 2—On the second day of the new year, good luck dolls, *daruma*, are sold. The dolls have no eyes, but one is painted on when a wish is made, and another is added if the wish comes true.

Tamaseseri, Ball-Catching Day, January 3—Boys try to catch a sacred ball thrown by a priest at a shrine. The lucky recipient will have good luck all year.

The new year's celebration continues for an entire week, traditionally ending on *Nanakusa* when a dish of rice and herbs of the same name is served.

Hina Matsuri, Doll Festival, March 3-4—On this special day friends and families extend their good wishes for the health and happiness of girls. To observe the 1,000-year-old festival, young girls dress up and invite their friends to see their elaborate doll collections which have been displayed especially for the occasion. These dolls are not to be hugged or cuddled; in fact, no one would even want to touch them. They are very expensive, and many are priceless heirlooms passed down through generations. The costumes, some painted, others sewn of fabric, represent clothing of the Imperial Court. The displays also include intricate accessories, such as matchbox-sized chests of drawers, musical instruments, carriages, or tables set with artificial foods.

Kodomo-No-Hi, Children's Day, May 5—Originally this day was *Tango-No-Sekku* or Boy's Day and was dedicated to the boys of Japan. Now this national holiday centers on all children, but it is especially observed by families with male heirs. Giant paper carp (*koinobori*) are flown from tall poles, representing the strength of manhood. The largest koinobori flies highest on the pole, and smaller ones below coincide with the ages of the family's sons.

O-bon, Festival of the Dead, July 13-16— The commemorative day for the deceased is of Buddhist origin, based on the belief that one's ancestors return to earth during this time. To honor them the graves are swept and decorated, the home is cleaned, and offerings of food are set beside the family altar. Small fires might be lit to help guide the spirits of the ancestors from the world of the dead. Lighted lanterns are floated on rivers, symbolizing their return to earth. *O-bon* is a time for family reunion, and since Japanese workers are on vacation in August, it is more frequently celebrated then, when the entire family can be together.

Other special holidays and festivals include:

Adults' Day, January 15—A day to honor all the young people who have reached 20, the age at which they can vote.

Hana Matsuri, Flower Festival, April 8—Buddha's birthday is celebrated with services at most temples.

Tanabata, Star Festival, July 7—This festival commemorates the romantic legend of two lovers who were forbidden to meet except once a year. They are represented by two stars whose paths cross the Milky Way on this night.

Keiro-No-Hi, Respect for the Aged Day, September 15—On this day the elderly of the family are honored.

Shichi-Go-San, Children's Shrine Visiting Day, November 15—Children are dressed in their best clothing and taken to the shrine where those who are ages 7, 5, and 3 are honored. Prayers are offered for good health and success.

Overview

The Western concept of religion involves a set of doctrines incorporating the existence of an omnipotent being or supernatural powers that determine the fate of people and nature. This concept may not be applicable in the Asian world where religion usually encompasses all aspects of life for individuals as well as for social groups. At the same time, there is little or no difference between what is sacred and what is secular. In Asia, there are a multitude of religions—from exalted schemes of mysticism to diverse superstitions and beliefs.

Asian religions might be categorized very simply into two main groups: regional religions and universal religions. The first category refers to certain ethnic or indigenous groups of people such as India's Hinduism, Japan's Shintoism, and China's Taoism and Confucianism. The second category includes Buddhism, Islam, and Christianity. These are universal religions in that each holds that the religious meaning of life and the world cannot be achieved by a limited number of people or cultures.

Unlike Western religions, Asian religions—regional and universal— have crossed paths throughout history, resulting in their subtle transformation. The ranks of Asian spiritualism include philosophical men such as the Buddha, Confucius, and Gandhi, as well as fierce warriors who plundered the lands, such as Genghis Khan and Tamerlane. Asians have preserved their spiritual views despite the many upheavals throughout the ages. The religious history of Japan provides a good example of traditional ways mingling with new ones.

Shintoism

Shinto, the traditional Japanese religion, has undergone many changes due to the influence of Confucianism, Buddhism, and other religions. Nevertheless, Shinto has always been important to the religious, cultural, and national life of Japan.

The myth of the Imperial Family's divine origin goes back to the most important deity, the Sun Goddess Amaterasu, who is enshrined in the Grand Shrine of Ise. Scattered throughout Japan are nearly 80,000 other shrines. While Shinto has no sacred scriptures like most major religions, some of its basic tenets are found in two eighth century writings, the *Kojiki* (Records of Ancient Matters) and the *Nihonshoki* (Chronicles of Japan). According to the Shinto mythologies, in the beginning gods married goddesses and out of these unions came the mountains, rivers, seas, plants, animals, humans, and numerous other deities.

Shinto does not focus on doctrines. However, it does assert the basic goodness of human nature and of the world. Evil in Shinto is little more than a lack of beauty and harmony. Moreover, good can be re-established by ceremonial cleansing. Shinto, which is a communal religion, stresses the cooperative efforts and celebrations of the family clan, village, and nation on holy days and public festivals, instead of individual beliefs and decisions. Religious practice centers on the worship of *Kami*: spirits, forces of nature, or departed ancestors strong enough to help or harm in rice farming, sickness, and all other human problems, as well as heroes, emperors, and a few scholars. In contrast to the

United States Constitution's separation of church and state, Shinto professes that religion and the state are inseparable.

Buddhism

In the middle of the sixth century, Buddhism (imported from Korea) brought changes in basic religious beliefs. The previous religion had been a blend of animism and earth religions of the agricultural tribes in Japan. After the introduction of Buddhism, called the way of the Buddha, the previously unlabeled religion was named Shinto, the way of the gods. After gaining imperial favor, Buddhism spread throughout the country and superseded Shintoism in some places for centuries.

Prince Siddhartha

Although often identified as a Japanese religion, Buddhism is an import from India, by way of China and Korea over the course of many centuries. The religion's founder was Prince Siddhartha (also known as Gautama and Sakyamuni). He was a minor prince, born near the present-day India-Nepal border about five centuries B.C. He was a close contemporary of Confucius. Reared in royal Indian tradition, he trained as a warrior, married, and fathered a son. Despite his privileged existence, he was greatly troubled by the human pain and suffering he observed all around him. As a result, he abandoned his comfortable life and sought spiritual happiness. At the age of 36, after many years of contemplation, he finally attained enlightenment, gaining the title "Buddha," "Enlightened." He spent the remaining 45 years of his life spreading his teachings in northern India. Buddhist tenets are based on the belief that all of life is filled with pain, anguish, and suffering caused by mankind's craving for impermanent things. Salvation, or nirvana, can be gained only when people eliminate the causes of suffering by following physical, mental, and spiritual disciplines. Buddhist doctrine, philosophy, art, and extensive scriptures developed from the humble preachings of a corps of lay teachers.

Saicho and Kukai

In Japan, during the Heian Period (794-1185 A.D.), Buddhism took on a new dimension thanks to the work of two great monks, Saicho (767-822 A.D.) and Kukai (744-839 A.D.). They made pilgrimages to China and each introduced a new religious sect. Saicho imported Tendai, and Kukai established Shingon. The diversity of Buddhism from its earliest times is comparable to Christian sectarianism.

Blending of Religions

Early in the ninth century Japanese Buddhism entered a new age, catering mainly to court aristocrats and contributing to the cultural growth of the nation. In the nineteenth century, many features of Buddhist beliefs and practices were assimilated into Shinto and vice versa. For example, today each Buddhist temple in Japan has a Shinto shrine somewhere on its grounds, and Shinto shrines have Buddhist altars. Most Japanese homes include ritual equipment from both religions: a miniature Shinto shrine and a Buddhist altar. Often Buddhist and Shinto gods seem interchangeable. There is a saying that every Japanese is born, named, and married with Shinto ceremonies, conducts himself as a Confucian, dies and is memorialized as a Buddhist. By contrast, although Western

Christianity originally combined diverse elements, once those elements had been assimilated, Christianity became exclusive; practices of other faiths were not permitted.

Cultural Influence

The period between 1336 and 1573 is considered the "Golden Age of Zen Buddhism." Its influence, however, was cultural rather than religious. Much of what non-Japanese people would identify readily as Japanese culture can be traced to this period. Zen, more than any other Buddhist sect, has received much publicity, reflecting its great intellectual and aesthetic appeal to Japanese and non-Japanese people alike.

Beginning in the Edo or Tokugawa Period (1600-1868), seeds of a strong nationalistic movement began to take root. Japanese leaders used Confucianism to encourage the study of Japanese history and other indigenous topics. Scholars of the nationalistic Shinto school known as *Kokugaku*, or "national learning," insisted on the superiority of Shinto thought over all imported teachings, including Buddhism. Thus the vitality of Buddhism was largely lost. The social and political power of Buddhist monasteries and temples began to decline. Also lost was the religion's cultural influence amidst the peace and comparative material security gained under the shogunate's strong governmental control.

New Religions

By the time of the Meiji Restoration (1868-1912), the government was ready to issue an edict distinguishing Shinto from Buddhism. From that time to the end of World War II, Shinto was a *de facto* state religion with shrines receiving government subsidies. Immediately after World War II, under the U.S. occupation, "State Shinto" was dismantled and Shinto shrines lost their government support. As a result, many small shrines or shrines lacking strong private support were forced to close.

Since the conclusion of World War II, new religions have gained momentum. Some are based on Shinto while others are related to certain sects of Buddhism.

Today, under the present Japanese Constitution, Shinto has no official status. Nevertheless, it continues to play ceremonial and symbolic roles in many aspects of Japanese life.

Confucianism

Under the rule of the Yamato Court in the fourth century, Chinese influence in the form of Confucianism began to be felt in Japan. Like Buddhism, Confucianism was also imported by way of Korea. Confucianism is a Western label. East Asians refer to it as "the teaching of the scholars."

Confucianism represents the teachings and traditions of Confucius, the K'ung-fu-tzu of Master Kung, who lived from 551 to 479 B.C. He was a teacher by profession, holding a minor government position in his province. Living in an unsettled and decadent time, he felt compelled to initiate social reform based on his ideas of moral philosophy. His efforts were unsuccessful, but his teachings left lasting influences on Chinese and later Japanese society.

Although Confucius did not pretend to be a messiah, a prophet, or even a philosopher, he transfused tradition with a new spirit. He believed anyone could be educated to understand the "Will of Heaven." Basic Confucian teaching centers on the harmonious conduct of five relationships: father and son, ruler and subject, husband and wife, elder and younger brothers, and friend and friend. Being family-oriented, Confucianism stresses the virtue of filial piety, the cult of ancestor worship, semi-religious ethics, the strict observation of proper social ritual, and etiquette.

Confucianism is less a religion than a system of morals, ethics, and politics based on loyalty, duty, and obedience. It centers on the idea of a family whose father—emperor—is the head. These elements have been observed throughout Japan's history, although its influence has declined since World War II.

Christianity

Christianity was the last major world religion to appear on the Asian scene. It has had a checkered history in Asia. The first recorded contact with Japan goes as far back as the sixteenth century when Portugal was expanding its overseas empire in Asia. In 1542, Francis Xavier (1506-1552), the Jesuit, arrived at Goa, India, and from there carried on a missionary campaign in Japan. In 1549, Spanish Jesuits brought Christianity to the shores of Japan, where it flourished. At this time of internal strife and upheaval the new religion was welcomed by those who wished to gain trade benefits or new Western technology, especially advanced firearms.

With the unification of the nation under the Tokugawa reign, however, the authorities suppressed all avenues for further change and banned Christianity in 1589 as subversive to the established order. They feared Spain or Portugal would colonize Japan as they had other countries throughout the world. The ban was in effect until the Meiji Era (1868).

In the modern period, Christian missionary activities in Asia followed the expansionist moves of European colonial powers. In the last 100 years, however, many European and American missionaries (both Catholic and Protestant) have established their evangelistic, educational, and philanthropic endeavors across their national boundaries. In recent decades, the emergence of the indigenous Christian churches in just about every part of Asia, including Japan, has been significant. Christianity is still not free from the label "foreign," unlike Buddhism and Confucianism. However, Japanese Christians, like other Christians in Asia, are taking an increasingly active part in social, cultural, and political life of their own nation. Among Japanese Christians today, Protestants and Catholics are about equal in number.

In all Asian countries (except the Philippines—the only Christian Asian country), the Christian population remains very small. Nevertheless, the Christian influence on Japanese society in modern times has been very great. As a group, Japanese Christians rank among the best-educated leaders in society and have had a disproportionate amount of influence on their fellow citizens. Also, because it is an important element in Western civilization, Christianity has attracted much interest and curiosity. Educated Japanese probably have a clearer understanding of Christian history and Christian dogma than they do of Buddhism, since Christianity probably would have been part of their course of study of significant world influences. Buddhism normally would not be included. The ability of the Japanese to accept and to assimilate foreign religious influences often astounds Western religious practitioners, whose religious practices are exclusive rather than inclusive.

Sports and Recreation

Japanese people enjoy both Western sports and traditional Japanese sports.

Western Sports

Baseball is called Japan's "national pastime." Introduced by two Americans in 1872, the game today attracts millions of avid fans, young and old. Two professional baseball leagues—Pacific and Central—have six teams; the league champions meet in the fall for the "Japan Series," an event as important to Japanese baseball fans as America's World Series. Rules are almost identical to those used in the United States, although the ball-parks tend to be slightly smaller and infields are made of packed dirt rather than turf. The season is 130 games long.

Some Japanese baseball teams have spring training camps in the United States, and a number of American ballplayers now play on Japanese teams. The best pitchers and batters in both leagues are well-known among children. If every American schoolchild knows Babe Ruth, all Japanese youths have heard of Sadaharu Oh, Japan's home run king who holds the world record—868 homers. He retired from the Tokyo Giants in 1980.

On hot summer evenings it is not uncommon for groups of friends to go to the ballpark for a *naitah* (night game), where they might eat *hotsutto dogu* (hot dogs) and watch the *sutoraiku* and *boru* (strikes and balls).

Other popular sports include volleyball, table tennis, tennis, swimming, boxing, wrestling, skiing, skating, basketball, hockey, gymnastics, and track and field. American football, soccer, and rugby have become popular recently among high school and university students. Golf is a favorite recreational sport among businessmen. Even in crowded Tokyo, where space is extremely limited, virtually every neighborhood has a driving range, where golfers can practice teeing off at targets in a screened-in field. Many Japanese also enjoy sailing, hiking, camping, and fishing.

Japanese Sports

The traditional Japanese sports include *karate, judo, kendo, kyudo,* and *sumo* wrestling.

Sumo is unique to Japan and is a favorite spectator sport, both at the ring and for television viewers. Six tournaments are held annually for sellout audiences. As in other Japanese arts, rituals and rules are part of this sport; the enormous combatants, wearing only loincloths, stomp their feet, clap their hands, snort, and sprinkle salt on the ground to ward off evil spirits before they begin their struggle. Though the warm-up of audience and wrestlers may take several minutes, the match itself may be very brief— usually less than one minute. A player loses if any part of his body, except his feet, touches the mat, or if he is forced out of the ring. The wrestlers are large—most weigh between 250 to 300 pounds—extremely agile, speedy, and strong.

Kendo, the art of fencing, originated around the seventh or eighth century, but it flourished during the sixteenth century when it became part of the martial training of samurai warriors. The *shinai*, a flexible bamboo sword, replaced the real swords used earlier. As in Western fencing, the offense attempts to touch the opponent in specific parts of the body in order to score points. Protective gear is worn by each player: face masks, torso guards, and gloves. Today kendo matches and training classes are held all over Japan.

Like kendo, karate, which means "empty hands," stresses mental and spiritual discipline in overcoming the opponent. But this self-defense sport is not as highly regarded as kendo. It is really a new sport, having been exported from Okinawa in the 1920s. The opponents spar with one another, adding a *kiai* or shout for emphasis. The two fighters are judged on the quality of this *kiai*, as well as on the quality and speed of the body movements.

Judo grew out of *jujutsu*, one of the traditional and deadly martial arts, originally practiced by the samurai. Most fighting in early Japan was on a one-to-one basis, and individual skill was crucial. Jujutsu was designed for unarmed defense, making it possible to disable or kill an opponent without a weapon.

During the period of the Tokugawa Shogunate, when there were no wars to fight, competitions developed between rival schools of martial arts. These tournament matches often resulted in serious injury and death. Later, in the nineteenth century, judo master Jigoro Kano modified jujutsu by eliminating its martial goals and developing it into a scientific system of discipline and training for mind and body. It was designated an Olympic sport in 1964.

Mass Media

Japanese mass media systems reflect the post-World War II phenomena that transformed this island nation into one of the most productive on earth.

As with most things in this war-devastated country, Japan's media arose from near destruction in 1945 to become within a few decades one of the largest, most technologically sophisticated and influential mass communications systems in the world.

By 1952, competition among the Japanese media intensified. By the early 1960s, the stage was set for phenomenal growth.

Contributing factors included the nation's economic expansion, a new constitution providing freedom-of-press guarantees similar in wording and intent to the U.S. First Amendment, new types of media and technology, and an emphasis on educational programming that has helped give Japan one of the world's highest literacy rates.

Newspapers

Today, two of Japan's Tokyo-based daily newspapers have the largest circulations in the world—the *Yomiuri Shimbun* with 14 million copies and the *Asahi Shimbun* with more than 12 million copies. Three of the world's top ten circulation leaders are Japanese, including the ninth place *Mainichi Shimbun* with a daily circulation of more than 7 million.

By comparison the newspaper with the largest daily circulation in the United States currently is the *Wall Street Journal* with 1.9 million copies.

The press systems that print the newspapers in Japan are the world's fastest. The *Yomiuri's* main plant in Tokyo has 90 press units, each capable of printing 130,000

24-page newspapers per hour. Its daily routine of 13 press runs includes 50,000 copies of an English-language evening edition.

Broadcast Journalism

The country also leads the way in broadcast journalism: Japan has programming different from anything yet developed in the United States.

For example, Japan's noncommercial organization, Nippon Hoso Kyokai (NHK), operates two TV channels, each with distinct programming patterns. As of 1986, NHK had 3,492 general broadcast stations, 2,416 educational stations and 2,573 stations with multiplex broadcasting. It also has 182 AM stations for general programming, 141 AM stations for educational programming, and 500 FM stations.

In addition, NHK maintains agreements with 29 broadcasting and related organizations in 22 countries for cooperation in coverage and satellite relays and exchanges of programs and technologies.

Reading and Viewing Habits

The reading and viewing habits of Japanese are equally impressive. In terms of the number of copies of daily newspapers purchased each day, Japan ranks highest in the world with 569 copies per 1,000 people. By comparison, the United States ranks ninth with 265 copies per 1,000 people.

Japan, with a total population of about 120 million, consumes more than 68 million newspapers daily. The total for the United States, with a population of about 235 million, is about 63 million newspapers.

Reading habits differ, too. The average Japanese spends more than 40 minutes each day reading his or her newspaper; the average American spends about 20 minutes a day with his or her newspaper.

In Japan, economic news is the most widely read category of news. Because of Japan's reliance on importing raw materials and exporting finished goods, news of international developments is also of great interest.

Programming

Political developments within Japan, the dominance of the ruling Liberal Democratic Party, the appreciating value of the yen and its impact on world trade and domestic spending, and concerns over higher education all receive significant attention from the media. Surprisingly, as popular as competitive sports are in Japan, they receive comparatively little media attention. The exception is the annual Grand Sumo wrestling tournament, which is less a competitive sport than a celebration of ancient symbolism.

Perhaps NHK's noncommercial operations provide the most marked contrast between Japan and the United States in terms of television programming. The organization's Channel 1 devotes 38 percent of its 18-hour broadcasting day to news, 27 percent to culture, 22 percent to entertainment and 13 percent to education.

Its Channel 3 devotes 2 percent to news, 20 percent to culture and 78 percent to education. Many of the educational programs are on learning a foreign language, especially English or Russian.

Commercial television programming is similar to that in the United States except that more of it is locally produced and more time is devoted to news. One commercial station has an 80-minute evening news program divided about equally between international, national and local (Tokyo) news.

Perhaps because of its highly industrialized society, its unique and strategic position in the world scheme of things, or its own individuality, Japan has created in the post-World War II period what it proudly has called "an informationalized society" unlike any other in the world.

Merritt Christensen is associate professor of journalism at the University of Wisconsin-Eau Claire and was visiting professor of journalism at Sophia University, Tokyo, during spring semester 1987. This article, which appeared in the Eau Claire *Leader Telegram*, January 31, 1988, is condensed from Christensen's research on the Japanese news media and is reprinted with the consent of the author.

References

Bisignani, J.D. *Japan Handbook*. Moon Publications, 1983.

DeMente, Boye. *The Whole Japan Book*. Phoenix Books, 1983.

In Search of Mutual Understanding: A Classroom Approach to Japan. Bloomington, IN: Social Studies Development Center, Indiana University, 1985.

Japan. Oklahoma Department of Education, 1983.

"Living Arts," *Video Letter from Japan*. The Asia Society, 1984.

"My Day," *Video Letter from Japan*. The Asia Society, 1986.

Putzar, Edward. *Japanese Literature: A Historical Outline*. University of Arizona Press, 1973.

"Seasons," *Video Letter From Japan*. The Asia Society, 1985.

What I Want to Know About Japan. Japan Information Center, 1983.

Activities: Culture 4

Folktales of Japan: Role-Playing for Primaries

Activity 1: **Elementary Level, K-1**

These are sample activities, or examplars, only. They can be used as described or re-modeled to suit local needs. They also may suggest ideas for additional folktale experiences for elementary students.

Objectives

● To become familiar with and enjoy folktales used in elementary schools in Japan
● To use folktales as a motivator for role-playing
● To locate Japan on the map or globe and become aware of its status as a nation

Materials

● *Urashima Taro and Other Japanese Children's Stories*, edited by Florence Sakade

Suggested Procedures

1. Read or tell several of the short folktales in *Urashima Taro* (or a similar collection).
2. Ask children to talk about their favorite stories and decide which one to dramatize.
3. Select role-playing participants and a narrator from volunteers.
4. Help the narrator and the actors by reviewing the background and sequence of events of the chosen story. Such questions might include:
   Q. Where does the story take place?
   A. Far away in a land called Japan.
   Q. When did it happen?
   A. A long time ago . . . before you were born.
   Q. What did the old man find?
   A. A small mortar made of stone.
   Q. What happened when he took it home?
   A. His brother stirred the mortar with the stick and rice came out of it!
5. Encourage the narrator and the actors to continue the story, prompting when necessary, and bring the play to a conclusion.
6. Select another group of students to re-enact the story. Usually, this group will need less prompting.

Follow-Up Activities

1. Make up a song or chant that can be added to the folktale.
2. Draw pictures of the characters and events and compile a booklet, adding text as told by the children.
3. Construct simple paper-bag masks for each of the characters in the folktale.
4. Locate Japan on a globe and map. On a world map, look for Wisconsin, the United States, and Japan. Discuss the idea that the United States is a nation, just as Japan is a nation. Japanese children have favorite folktales; which ones might be considered favorites of American children?

Folktales of Japan: Role-Playing for Primaries

Questions for Discussion

1. Who are the people of our land and other lands?

2. What needs do all people have?

3. What do girls and boys do in other lands?

4. What do families everywhere do together?

Visiting a Japanese Home

Activity 2: Elementary Level, 2-4

These are sample activities, or examplars, only. They can be used as described or re-modeled to suit local needs. They also may suggest ideas for additional cultural experiences for elementary students.

Objectives

- To become familiar with Japanese home life and customs
- To learn selected Japanese vocabulary about home life
- To compare homes and customs in Japan with those in Wisconsin

Materials

- Activity Sheet 1: You Are Invited to Yuki's House
- Activity Sheet 2: Japanese and English Words
- Activity Sheet 3: A Comparison Story
- Activity Sheet 4: Crossword Puzzle
- *A Family in Japan* by Judith Elken

Suggested Procedures

1. Read "You Are Invited to Yuki's House" together in class.
2. Using Japanese and English words found on Activity Sheet 2, each student will write comparable English terms for the Japanese words. The class can practice saying the Japanese words together. Additional words might be added; see basic vocabulary list in this guidebook (pages 39-42).
3. Using Activity Sheet 3: A Comparison Story, each student will write a story introducing a Japanese child to their home and customs. They will want to consult their Japanese-English word list and the story as they write.
4. Make flashcards for the Japanese words in the story. After practicing and learning the words, students will use their new vocabulary in the crossword puzzle, Activity Sheet 4.

Follow-Up Activity

Have students write to Japanese pen pals, using this story to tell about life in a Wisconsin home. (See p. 178 in the Resource Section.)

Additional Easy Activities

1. Discover the background of the *chanouy* (tea ceremony), its significance in Zen Buddhism, its traditional setting, the elements of the ceremony. Let students share their findings through discussion or artistic renderings of the teahouse, the utensils, and the manners of the participants.

2. Make kimonos from large sheets of brown or white butcher paper. Decorate with appropriate designs using paints, crayons or felt-tipped markers. Tape or staple the pieces together at the shoulders and sleeves. Research about kimonos might include: appropriate colors for various occasions and seasons, designs and fabrics used, and costs of purchasing.

3. Bring ingredients from home and prepare a simple Japanese dish in an electric wok. A combination of vegetables and sliced chicken makes an excellent "stir-fry" and one that most children will like. *O cha* (green tea) or a soft drink can be served as a beverage. Through photographs and films children can learn that meal service and tableware are very carefully chosen and arranged in Japan. If Japanese items are not available for use in the classroom, paper plates and cups may be decorated with appropriate Japanese designs. Small bowls can be used for serving soup. Since no spoons are used, soup may be drunk directly from the bowl. The aesthetics of the meal are very important, so students may want to create a garden scene or arrange flowers for the occasion. In Japan it is rude to show hunger, and eating is a mannerly and polite experience. Eat the stir-fry dish with *hashi* (chopsticks).

4. After studying the Japanese *ikebana* (flower arranging) and gardening, collect tree or shrub branches and vases or other containers to use for simple arrangements. Weight the containers with sand, or use styrofoam blocks to sustain the arrangements. have students draw or collect pictures of Japanese arrangements or garden designs; mat these and add them to the branch arrangements for a "gallery" or art show.

Visiting a Japanese Home

You Are Invited to Yuki's House

This activity was provided by Charlotte Myhers, a fourth grade teacher at Osseo Elementary School, Osseo, Wisconsin; it was written by Noriko Sumigama, a Japanese intern at the school.

The most important place in Tokyo is the home of each person. Tokyo is a noisy, modern city. It has contemporary industry, department stores, and cars. On the other hand, the Japanese home is a quiet, simple place. It is a place of old customs, traditions, and polite manners.

Please come into Yuki's house. Yuki takes off her *getas*, sandals. You will please take off your shoes also and put on house slippers. Open the panel door, the *fusuma*, by sliding it to one side. You will notice its frame is covered with rice paper. This paper is called *shoji*. Please step up into Yuki's house.

Yuki's mother comes to greet you. She says, *Irrashai-mase*, meaning "welcome." You say, *Konnichiwa*, "hello," and present her with a small gift. The Japanese people often give each other gifts to show their friendship. The gift is never opened in front of the giver.

Please come into Yuki's *chanoma*, living room. You will notice mats on the floor. These are called *tatami*. Tatami are made of woven grass and rice straw. These mats are very soft and springy to walk on. Each room is measured by the number of tatami it contains. The chanoma has a low, square table in the middle of it. There are cushions on all sides, called *zabuton*. You are the guest of honor. You will be asked to sit near the *tokonoma*, the most important part of the chanoma. There is a scroll hanging there, with a picture or a poem on it. There is also an arrangement of flowers. Each season Yuki's mother changes the way of arranging the flowers. Yuki is learning how to do *ikebana*, flower arranging, at school.

The Japanese want to feel very close to nature. The wood in their houses is never painted. There is a garden in almost every home. Even the apartments have gardens on the balconies. The Japanese love flowers and trees.

Yuki will give you a light *kimono*, or *yukata*, to wear. A fine dinner is eaten with *hashi*, chopsticks. It is prepared in front of you. After dinner, the dishes are put away. Yuki brings out her games. They are lots of fun. You need to concentrate hard to play them.

There is time to watch a program on TV. Yuki loves to see the adventures of Quataro the ghost. There are many American shows on TV, too. It is funny for you to see the actors speaking Japanese. Yuki's brother, Yoshiro, plays baseball every chance he gets. He even plays in the winter. It is the favorite sport in Japan.

It is getting late! After you leave, Yuki's mother will move the table to one side and bring the *futon* out of the closet. Futons are mattresses. Most Japanese people sleep on futons, but some have beds like those found in Europe or North America.

You say *arigato gozaimasu*, "thank you," to Yuki's parents for sharing their way of life with you. *Sayonara*.

Visiting a Japanese Home

Japanese and English Words

	Japan	**Wisconsin**
	Yuki	_____
		(your name)
getas	(gay-tas)	_____
fusuma	(foo-soo-mah)	_____
shoji	(sho-jee)	_____
chanoma	(cha-noh-mah)	_____
tatami	(ta-tah-mee)	_____
zabuton	(za-boo-tahn)	_____
tokonoma	(toh-koh-noh-mah)	_____
ikebana	(ee-ke-bah-na)	_____
kimono	(kee-moh-noh)	_____
yukata	(yoo-kah-tah)	_____
futon	(foo-tahn)	_____

Visiting a Japanese Home

A Comparison Story

You Are Invited to _____ House
(your name)

The most important place in _____ is the home of each person.
(your town)

_____

_____

_____

_____

_____

_____

_____

_____

_____

_____

_____

_____

_____

Visiting a Japanese Home

Crossword Puzzle

Across

1. Flower arranging
2. Living room
4. Mattress
5. Quiet place with flowers and poem
8. Rice paper covering door frame
9. A light kimono
10. Sandals
12. Cushions around a square table

Down

1. "Welcome!"
3. Japanese eat with

_____.

6. Sliding panel door
7. "Hello!"
11. Floor mats of woven grass and rice straw

Directions

1. Read "You Are Invited to Yuki's House."
2. Make flash cards for the Japanese words in the story.
3. After you study the words on the flash cards, complete this crossword puzzle.

Solution appears on page 179.

67

Visiting a Japanese Home

Questions for Discussion

1. What are families like in other parts of the world?

2. In what ways do people adjust to the problems of urban community living?

3. In what ways is homelife in Wisconsin comparable to life in Japan?

Cultural Communication through Folktales

Activity 3: Intermediate Level, 4-7

This activity was contributed by Beth A. Elver, geography teacher, Oregon Junior High School, Oregon, Wisconsin.

These are sample activities, or examplars, only. They can be used as described or re-modeled to suit local needs. They also may suggest ideas for additional cultural experiences for intermediate students.

Objectives

● To introduce Japanese folktales that reflect Japanese culture and entertain the present generation of children

Materials

● *Japanese Children's Favorite Stories*. Florence Sakade, Charles E. Tuttle Company, Rutland, Vermont.
● Selected collections of Japanese folktales (For additional folktale titles, see p. 168 in the resources section of this guidebook.)
● Activity Sheet 1: Japanese Folktale Comparison and summary
● Activity Sheet 2: Questions for Discussion

Suggested Procedures

1. Teacher reads a Japanese folktale as an introduction and shows additional books of tales available in the school or public library.
2. Students will be given the Japanese Folktale Comparison activity sheets; each will choose two folktales from a selection of five or six.
3. The students will read their folktales and complete the assignment.

Follow-Up Activities

1. To encourage class participation the teacher might lead a charting activity to expand upon information gathered on the activity sheets.
2. The teacher might consider dividing the class into groups to prepare plays based on folktales.
3. Compare Japanese and American folktales with a common theme.

Additional Easy Activities

1. Construct puppets from tagboard and mount them on dowels or heavy cardboard to represent the characters in a Japanese folktale. Have students rewrite the story as a puppet skit, then practice performing it before inviting another class to watch it.

2. Provide an opportunity to do research on Kabuki. Older students may find the history of this drama form very interesting, especially because women were banned and their parts were given to male actors. Younger students might be interested in the elaborate costumes, masks, and unique staging. This complex and colorful art form should also provide opportunities for writing; for example, students may select a folktale incident, rewrite it into a skit, and present it using homemade Kabuki elements such as stringed instruments, masks, and chants. A helpful book: *The Kabuki Handbook* (A Guide to Understanding and Appreciation with Summaries of Favorite Plays, Explanatory Notes, and Illustrations) by Aubrey and Giovanna Halford, Tuttle, 1955. (Paperback available: $8.75)

Cultural Communication through Folktales

Japanese Folktale Comparison

Folktale 1	Folktale 2
Title	Title
Characters	Characters
Settings	Settings
Problems (at least 2)	Problems (at least 2)
Items Mentioned in Folktale	Items Mentioned in Folktale
Ending	Ending
What I'll Remember Most About this Folktale	What I'll Remember Most About this Folktale

Of the folktales I chose, I most enjoyed the one called, _____

because _____ .

The character in this folktale I would most like to meet is _____ .

I would like to ask him/her _____

_____ .

I think he/she would answer my question by saying _____

_____

_____

This folktale was different from the other folktales because _____

_____

_____ .

I think the most important item in this folktale is _____

because _____

_____ .

This folktale makes me think of the color _____

because _____

_____ .

One word that would describe this folktale is _____

because _____

_____ .

Cultural Communication through Folktales

Questions for Discussion

1. What factors shape culture?

2. How do people share their cultures with one another?

3. How are cultures like one another? How are they different?

Wisconsin and Japan: Similarities and Differences

Activity 4: Intermediate Level, 4-7

This activity was contributed by Beth A. Elver, geography teacher, Oregon Junior High School, Oregon, Wisconsin.

These are sample activities, or examplars, only. They can be used as described or remodeled to suit local needs. They also may suggest ideas for additional cultural experiences for elementary students.

Objectives

● To discover ways Wisconsin and Japan are similar and different

Materials

● *All-Japan: The Catalogue of Everything Japanese*, introduction by Oliver Statler, Quill, 1984; 105 Madison Avenue, New York, NY 10016.
● *Video Letters from Japan*, The Asia Society Education Department.
● *1990 World Almanac*
● Encyclopedias, atlases, and other general reference works
● Current newspaper/magazine articles
● Activity Sheet 1: Wisconsin–Japan: A Comparison
● Activity Sheet 2: Questions for Discussion

Suggested Procedures

1. Divide the class into small groups. Each group might be responsible for one or two of the areas of comparison on Activity Sheet 1: Wisconsin–Japan: A Comparison. Ask them to follow the directions on the sheet.
2. Groups will research their area(s) using the materials provided or additional ones.
3. Class discussion of the questions on Activity Sheet 2 might take the form of oral presentations by small groups, after each group has added its findings to the chart on Activity Sheet 1.

Additional Easy Activities

1. After learning about the traditional arts and crafts in Japan, do some research on crafts that are indigenous to the upper midwest, especially Wisconsin. Include crafts that show our state's diverse ethnicity: birchbark baskets, quilting, rosemaling, Hmong applique, boat-building, Ukrainian egg designs. (*Wisconsin Trails* magazine is a good source for this.) Prepare a museum display using small items from Japan (fans, dolls, lacquerware) and those made in Wisconsin. Information about the origin of the craft or item may accompany each piece. Invite another class (or parents and grandparents) in to view you exhibit.

2. Use books, periodicals, films, and reference materials to study the historical costumes of people from Japan and Wisconsin, then create lifesized characters from butcher paper. (Students can lie on the paper and trace one another for the basic form.) Use felt-tipped markers to color the characters with authentic costumes of the Winnebago, the Menominee, the Ojibwa, French explorers, European immigrants, samurai warriors, and emperors.

3. Prepare a display illustrating contrasts in Japan's and Wisconsin's celebrations. Regional festivals in Wisconsin might include the Applefest in Bayfield, the Birkebeiner Cross-Country Race in Cable, the Swiss Fest in New Glarus, and Syttende Mai in Stoughton. Japan's festivals might include Children's Day (May 5), the Bon Festival (July or August), and Peace Day (August 6). An international costume parade is fun.

Activity Sheet 1

Wisconsin and Japan: Similarities and Differences

Wisconsin—Japan: A Comparison

Directions: Use resources, such as books, encyclopedias, almanacs, atlases, newspapers, television, magazines, personal interviews, and video programs to find information on the following topics relating to life in Wisconsin and Japan. How are we more alike than different? How are we more different than alike?

Wisconsin	Japan
Clothing	Clothing
Communication	Communication
Education	Education
Family Activities	Family Activities
Food	Food

Wisconsin	Japan
Homes	**Homes**
Jobs	**Jobs**
Leisure Time Activities	**Leisure Time Activities**
Transportation	**Transportation**
Miscellaneous	**Miscellaneous**

Wisconsin and Japan: Similarities and Differences

Questions for Discussion

1. What is culture?

2. What kinds of things are universal to all cultures?

3. How are cultures similar to and different from one another?

4. How can a person compare cultures?

Cultural Comparisons Through Media

Activity 5: Intermediate Level, 7-9

These are sample activities, or examplars, only. They can be used as described or re-modeled to suit local needs. They also may suggest ideas for additional cultural experiences for elementary students.

Objectives

- To use a variety of media to explore cultural contrasts in contemporary Japan and the United States
- To practice using the *Reader's Guide to Periodical Literature*, the card catalog, and the vertical file to find appropriate media
- To develop an appreciation for the unique characteristics of Japanese and American cultures

Materials

- Research materials may be collected prior to class. These might include articles from education and business journals, newspaper articles, and pamphlets about Japan.
- Films, videocassettes, and filmstrips. Our reviewers have suggested two helpful resources: *A Half Step Behind: Japanese Women of the Eighties*, by Jane Condon, Dodd-Mead, 1985; *Women in Japan* (filmstrip and audiocassette), by Majorie Bingham and Susan Gross, Glenhurst Publications.
- Indexes such as *The Reader's Guide to Periodical Literature, National Geographic Index*, and other materials are available in the instructional media center.
- Activity Sheet 1: The Role of Women
- Activity Sheet 2: Attitudes About Work
- Activity Sheet 3: Care of the Elderly

Suggested Procedures

1. Divide the class into small work groups and distribute study guides on several topics.
2. Additional topics may be added, such as education, crime, or religion.
3. Class will search for appropriate information, make notes on their findings, and prepare to discuss their findings.
4. Class discussion may center on oral presentations by small groups, or information might be presented on large charts which the groups have prepared.

Follow-Up Activities

Invite a native Japanese to visit the class, asking him or her to discuss the questions students researched. Consider this question: Does a firsthand account agree with media accounts?

Additional Easy Activities

1. Prepare a classroom dictionary of important words and phrases, showing each in English and Japanese. After duplicating these pages for each class member, have individuals design their own cover using Japanese-style art and calligraphy and laminate the cover with clear plastic. Practice using simple words and phrases in Japanese on a daily basis.

2. With a small group, design a Japanese newspaper. Use some Japanese words, if possible, or a few symbols with translations. The newspaper might include articles about travel in Japan, the current value of the yen, U.S.-Japan trade relations, reviews about new Japanese materials in the school library, a movie review, Haiku poetry, advertisements of Japanese products, comics, puzzles, and recipes for Japanese dishes. Design a cover or headlines with some calligraphy or Japanese crests. Duplicate the newspaper and distribute it to other classes.

3. Learn about some of Japan's great shrines or other favorite sites. Using references, such as travel magazines, tourist brochures, and reference books, design postcards or travel posters to advertise Japan. Include some written information about the specific site or shrine, where it is located, facts about the climate, and history of the area.

4. Using costume ideas from Japanese stories and folktales, as well as other sources, design paper dolls for a Doll Festival (*Hina Matsuri*). Label the dolls with the era or occupation they represent (for example, woman from the Meiji Period, or Kabuki dancer). Arrange the dolls in a pyramidal display and invite others to come to learn about the origins and traditions of Hina Matsuri.

5. Compare a Japanese newspaper to your hometown newspaper. Use the inquiry method. Show the students your hometown newspaper. Ask: What is this? Why do people read the paper? What can you find out about in the newspaper? List their responses on the chalkboard (e.g., sports, weather, TV schedule, advertisements, horoscope, comics, news). Show them the foreign paper. Take the pages apart and give a page to small groups of students to explore for five minutes. (The teacher may want to laminate these pages for continued use.) Bring the whole class back together. Did anyone find something listed on the chalkboard? You may also discuss types of products advertised, their cost, and Japan's monetary system. What sports appeared popular? Have someone explain a cartoon. Did they recognize anyone in the photos (president, rock star, movie star)?

Cultural Comparisons Through Media

The Role of Women

As you look at cultural similarities and differences between Japan and the United States consider the following questions. Feel free to add more if you find further significant information.

1. In each country, what role do women play in household management?

2. The idea of freedom or women's rights may be interpreted differently in other cultures. For example, in Japan a married woman's idea of freedom might be *not* accompanying her husband to a dinner party where his business partners gather. What would be the corresponding norms in American culture? What other notions of women's rights could be contrasted in Japanese and American cultures?

3. What kind of career goals are sought by American and Japanese women?

4. If an American woman were working for a firm in Japan, would she be able to realize her goal of seeking a management job? What obstacles might she have to face?

Cultural Comparisons Through Media

Attitudes About Work

As you look at cultural similarities and differences between Japan and the United States consider the following questions. Make additional comments if you find further significant information.

1. What is meant by the American Protestant work ethic? Is this idea still prevalent in the United States? Is there a work ethic in Japan?

2. What differences are there between Japanese and American work weeks? Between vacations?

3. How do attitudes about work, especially in the corporate business world, affect family life in Japan?

4. Contrast the Japanese and American attitudes about the role of labor unions and resolving conflict between management and labor.

Cultural Comparisons Through Media

Care of the Elderly

As you look at cultural differences and similarities between Japan and the United States, consider the following questions. Feel free to add more if you find further significant information.

1. What contrasts do you find between American and Japanese attitudes about caring for grandparents? What might be the historical background for these attitudes?

2. How do the roles of eldest sons differ in the two societies?

3. Consider the geography of the two countries, the contrasts in job mobility, the history of immigration in the United States. How might these factors affect attitudes about caring for older relatives?

4. What festivals or other commemorations in Japanese and American cultures show reverence for the elderly?

Government, Education, and Society

5

Government

Since 1946, Japan has had a democratic system of government with power shared by three branches—legislative, executive, and judicial. As in the United States, these branches act as checks and balances for one another.

The emperor is a symbol of state, but holds no governmental powers. This role is defined by the Constitution and includes such tasks as addressing and persuading the Legislature and awarding honors. This role has changed drastically from the days when an emperor was considered to be a deity.

The Diet

The legislative branch, known as the national Diet, is the highest and most powerful organ of state. Similar to the Congress of the United States, it is responsible for drafting laws, initiating constitutional revisions, making budgetary decisions, approving treaties, and designating a prime minister.

The House of Representatives, whose members are elected for four-year terms, has 511 seats; the House of Chancellors, whose representatives are elected for six-year terms, has 252 seats. As of 1986, nine political parties were represented in the Diet. In both houses the majority of the seats are held by the Liberal Democratic Party, Japan's major conservative political group. Other parties represented are the Japanese Socialist Party, the Komei Party, the Democratic Socialist Party, the Japan Communist Party, and several others with more limited representation.

Members of the Diet are elected directly by the people, all of whom are guaranteed the right to vote by the Constitution upon reaching the age of 20.

The Executive Branch

The executive branch of Japan's government is comprised of the prime minister and 20 ministers of state who are collectively called the Cabinet. The prime minister is a member of the Diet and is chosen by his colleagues in the Diet. He serves in this role until he chooses to resign or loses the Diet's vote of confidence. The responsibilities of the Cabinet include administration of law and affairs of state, management of foreign affairs, conclusion of treaties, administration of civil service, and preparation of the budget.

The Judicial Branch

The judiciary consists of five categories: the Supreme Court, high courts, district courts, family courts, and summary courts. They are independent of the executive and legislative branches of government. As in the United States, the lower courts handle civil, domestic, and criminal cases. Juvenile cases (involving individuals under 20 years of age) are tried in family courts. The Supreme Court, presided over by 15 justices, is the court of final resolution.

Local Government

Whereas the national government is responsible for defense, foreign policy, and justice, local governments are in charge of matters related to land, disaster prevention, pollution control, labor, education, social welfare, and health. Coordination of activities between two or more municipalities is conducted by prefectural governments, the equivalent of county governments in the United States.

Local governments operate autonomously, with the chief executive officers being elected directly by the resident voters. The local assemblies also elected by popular vote decide on matters such as ordinances, budgets, and revenues.

Revenues come both from the municipalities and from the state and are based on population and economic development.

Government

Government Organization of Japan (1986)

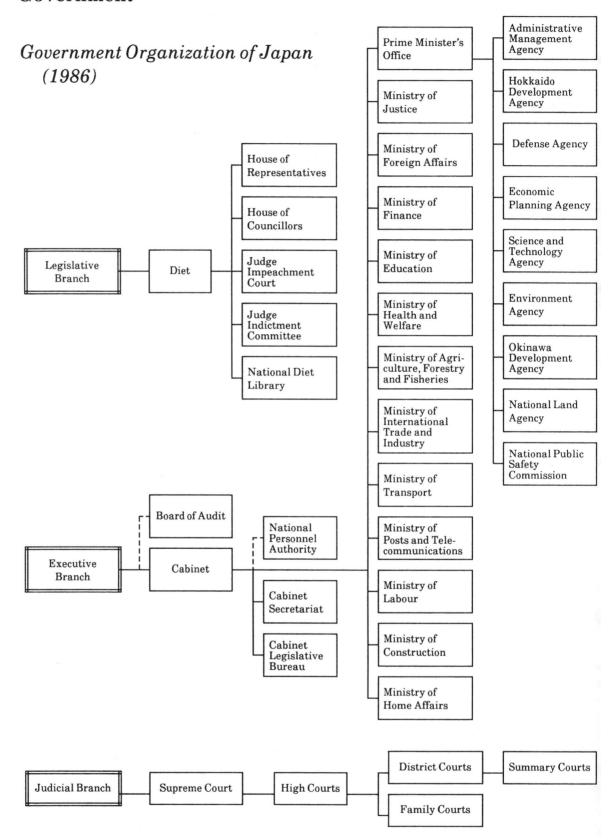

Source: *Statistical Handbook of Japan 1986*. Statistics Bureau, Management, and Coordinator Agency, 1986. p. 147.

Government

Prefectures of Japan

Aichi	25	Hyogo	17	Miyagi	41	Shimane	15
Akita	44	Ibaraki	39	Nagano	27	Shizuoka	26
Aomori	45	Ishikawa	30	Nagasaki	3	Tochigi	38
Chiba	35	Iwate	42	Nara	20	Tokushima	10
Chime	8	Kagawa	9	Niigata	32	Tokyo	34
Fukui	29	Kagoshima	7	Oita	5	Tottori	16
Fukuoka	1	Kanagawa	33	Okayama	14	Toyama	31
Fukushima	40	Kochi	11	Osaka	18	Wakayama	21
Gifu	24	Kumamoto	4	Saga	2	Yamagata	43
Gumma	37	Kyoto	19	Saitama	36	Yamaguchi	12
Hiroshima	13	Mie	22	Shiga	23	Yamanashi	28
Hokkaido	46	Miyazaki	6				

89

Government

Political Regions

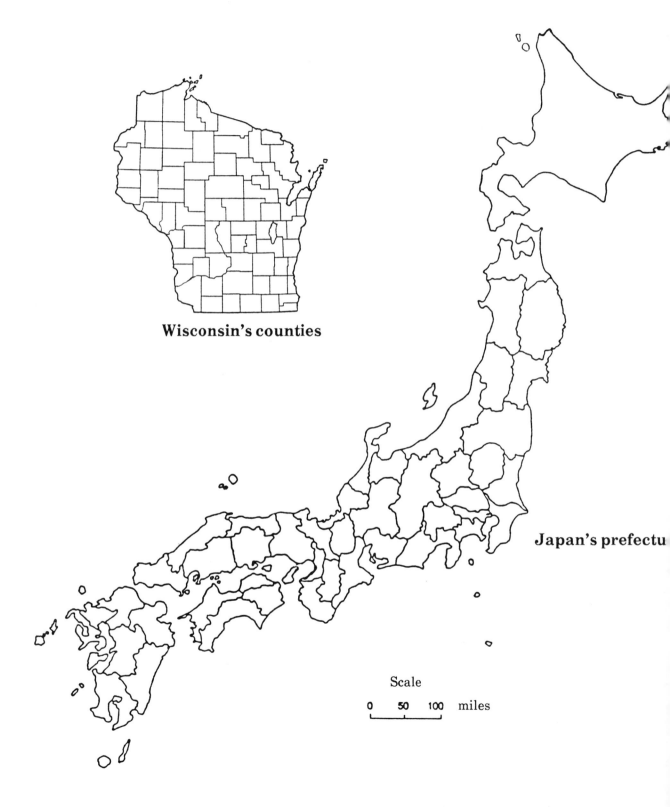

Wisconsin's counties

Japan's prefectu

Scale

0   50   100   miles

Education in Japan

The strong roots of education in Japan date back to the sixth and seventh centuries, when talented young Japanese went to China for schooling and brought back the best that Chinese culture had to offer.

During Japan's feudal period, schools were established to teach the children of the military class (samurai) the cultural, moral, and martial subjects necessary for fulfilling their duties as samurai warriors. Temple schools also were set up to teach reading, writing, and arithmetic to farmers and townspeople who needed such skills in their daily lives.

In the Meiji Era, the government established an integrated educational system, from elementary school to university levels, to foster the development of industry and culture through the introduction of Western learning. Equal education for all individuals became the basic tenet; the Education Act of 1872 stated that no communities should have illiterate persons.

The Value of Education

The Japanese continue to value education strongly. Article 26 of the Japanese Constitution states: "All people shall have the right to receive an equal education correspondent to their ability . . . . All people shall be obligated to have all boys and girls under their protection receive ordinary education." In practice this means free and compulsory education for everyone.

In addition, the Japanese may pursue other educational opportunities, such as vocational and technical training, international exchanges, classes via radio and television, or private schooling, like the *juku* schools which provide supplementary classes.

Teachers are respected in Japan; they are considered part of the *sensei*, "first born." They are well-trained, well-paid, and encouraged to advance in their careers since teaching is seen as a lifetime investment. Although American teachers may be well-trained in *how* to teach, Japanese teachers, especially at the upper grades, specialize in *what* they teach.

The *Monbusho*, the Ministry of Education, Science, and Culture, exercises tight control over the country's educational direction, regulating general curriculum, course content, textbooks, and schedule. Because of this, schools are uniform throughout the nation, although critics say this uniformity is a shortfall in Japan's otherwise commendable educational system.

Competition and Coaching

Japanese schools do face some problems: overcrowded classrooms and fierce competition among secondary students vying for places in the best schools and colleges. Students attend special preparatory schools or have tutors help them prepare for the entrance exams. This coaching is given after school, leaving most school children with little leisure time. Students who do poorly on their exams have little hope of continuing an academic career. The pressure to succeed on high school and university entrance exams is extreme and even has led to suicides.

The Japanese family plays an extremely important role in education. Because most mothers do not work full-time, they help their children through the rigors of education, from infancy through high school exams. The *kyoiku mama*, super mom, will teach her preschooler numbers and letters; attend her childrens' classes if they are sick; take an active role in a PTA; and take classes in the courses her children are studying. Parents stress the seriousness of school, and ensure that their children have good study habits and complete their homework on time.

Elementary Through University

The Japanese school year lasts 240 days compared with about 180 days in U.S. schools. This includes Saturdays when classes run from 8:30 a.m. to noon.

Education begins for some children as early as age three, when they might attend half-day kindergartens. Compulsory education begins at age six, when children enter first grade, and lasts for nine years: six in elementary school and three in junior high school.

In elementary school, children learn basic subjects needed in daily life. Usually, one teacher teaches all the subjects for one class. Junior high students learn the basic knowledge and skills needed to work in their society. Their teachers teach different subjects.

After graduation from junior high school, students may find a job, go to high school, or attend vocational high school. In April 1980, 94 percent of junior high school graduates entered senior high schools or technical schools, while 37 percent of senior high school graduates went on to universities or junior colleges. Students must pass entrance exams to get into senior high school or college.

In senior high school, students study general academic or specialized subjects; English is often a graduation requirement. Most high schools are run by regional and local governments, while others are privately administered. In addition to their classwork, high school students must be involved in at least one extracurricular activity, such as karate, calligraphy, or the tea ceremony.

Of the options available after senior high, the Japanese choose among four-year universities, two-year junior colleges, specialized training schools, or employment.

Education in Japan

School Curriculum

Elementary School—1st – 6th

Japanese Language
Social Studies
Arithmetic
Science
Drawing and Handicrafts

Physical Education
Moral Education
Music
Home Economics (Fifth and Sixth Grade)
Special Activities
  • Karate
  • Calligraphy
  • Baseball

Junior High School—7th – 9th

Japanese Language
Social Studies—History and Geography
Mathematics
Science
Music and Fine Arts

Health and Physical Education
Industrial Arts and Home Economics
Moral Education
Special Activities
Elective Subjects
  • Music
  • Foreign Language
  • Economics

High School—10th – 12th

Japanese Language
Social Studies
  • Contemporary Society
  • Japanese History
  • World History
  • Geography
  • Politics
  • Economics
Mathematics
  • Basic Math
  • Algebra
  • Geometry
  • Basic Analysis
  • Science

Health and Physical Education
Music and Fine Arts
Foreign Language
Home Economics

Source: *Education in Japan: A Brief Outline*. Tokyo: Monbusho, Japanese Ministry of Education, Science, and Culture, p. 7.

Education in Japan

The Daily Life of Senior High Students in Japan

Written by Kanehide Seo, *The Life of a Senior High School Student.* Tokyo: International Society for Educational Information, 1986.

How do Japanese senior high students spend their time after school and on holidays?

First of all, they study. There seems to be a major difference between students who intend to advance to the university level and those who do not. According to a national survey, those who desire to continue their education spend 153 minutes per day studying, while students who choose to work spend 53 minutes per day. Third-year students who contemplate advancing to a university spend four to five hours per day or more studying after school.

In Japan, there are private cram schools for intensive teaching, called *juku* or *yobiko*, which prepare students for university entrance examinations. Some students attend these three or four times per week for two or three hours at a time. Most Japanese students plan to attend a university and therefore attend the cram schools. About 30 percent of second-year students attend these schools after school hours. As for myself, club activities leave me no time to do so. Those going to cram schools say, however, once you get used to going, it is not much of a burden.

The reason we senior high school students study so much is that university entrance exams are getting tougher and tougher. But it is amazing how humans can adapt themselves to new situations. Many who plan to take the entrance exams take the intensive preparation in stride, accepting that nothing can be done to change the situation. Some foreigners feel that the Japanese "exam war" is crazy, but the students take it rather calmly.

Outside of studying, television seems to be the most popular activity. Our generation is referred to as the TV generation. In Tokyo alone there are seven channels including the semi-governmental NHK, which has two channels. Broadcasts continue from early morning to about midnight. We are inundated with a flood of TV programs, many of which have few, if any, good qualities. Parents worry about the possible bad influences on high school students. TV viewing time among senior high school students averages about one and one-half hours daily; some students might sit in front of the box as much as three or four hours each day. Clearly, the time that students spend watching television takes away from their reading time.

How do Japanese high school students spend their Sundays? A poll of students answering this question reported the following:

- 55 percent do nothing in particular
- 35 percent shop
- 22 percent pursue other interests
- 18 percent play sports
- 10 percent watch movies or plays

Cities in Japan lack green areas and parks. Urban areas have little outdoor recreational space where people can spend the day doing simple things. Spending the day idly at home may reflect the meager space outdoors.

What sports are popular in Japan? They include baseball, tennis, volleyball, judo and kendo, swimming, skiing, skating, soccer, fishing, and bowling. Sports that senior high school students would like to do in the near future are mountain climbing, surfing, diving, yachting, and golf—all rather costly to pursue. The most popular sport in Japan is baseball. During the professional baseball season, games are broadcast daily. Each year, national senior high school baseball series are held in spring and summer, and these games are broadcast on television and radio. Japanese baseball fever is somewhat extreme, perhaps rivaling America's.

Returning to the survey of Sunday activities, the large percentage of shoppers is noteworthy. When asked what items they most wanted, boys listed: an automobile, motorcycle, video deck, color television, and stereo. Girls' replies included: stereo, clothes, and jewelry. The things desired by both boys and girls probably differ little from high school students of other industrialized countries. But obtaining these things is possible only if you have money. A Japanese student's budget mostly goes to cover necessities such as food and drink, books, magazines, writing materials, and records.

How much spending money do senior high students receive per month? Many receive less than 10,000 yen, the average being 7,000 to 8,000. I receive 7,000 yen, but actually spend about half that. I wish to buy a video deck, so I save about 3,000 yen a month. I have accumulated quite an amount, but the sum is far short of the 150,000 to 200,000 yen needed to buy a video deck. About 50 percent of senior high students save for something they want, the average amount being around 110,000 yen. Many denounce the present age as materialistic. Some adults say that we youngsters just waste money, but I think we are steady and serious savers, trying to get along well in a consumer society.

Education in Japan

The Daily Life of a Sixth-Grader in Tokyo

Reprinted with permission from Timothy Plummer, *Opening Doors: Contemporary Japan*, The Asia Society, 1979.

Hi, my name is Takano Haruo. I am 11 years old and live in Tokyo. I am in the sixth grade. Next year I shall enter junior high school, so I am preparing to take entrance exams for the best junior high schools. The students of these junior high schools will be chosen purely on the basis of test scores. If I get into a good junior high school, then I will have a better chance of getting into one of the best high schools, and this, of course, can lead to one of the top national universities. Almost all good jobs go to the graduates of these universities.

Let me tell you what my typical school day is like. My day starts at about seven a.m. I wash up and dress while Mother fixes my breakfast of rice, fish, and some salad greens. Usually I wear shorts to school. School starts at eight-thirty and ends at three. I ride the train to school. It is too far for me to use my bike. All of my books and pens and junk are in a sack that has straps so I can wear it on my back.

The subjects I take are much the same as yours, except that students planning to go into high school must take English in addition to Japanese. Our exams in English concentrate mostly on reading and writing, so speaking English is very difficult for me. I also take science and math. We learn how to swim and play many sports in our gym class. I like gym best of all. Lunch is at noon. Usually we bring our lunches from home. We eat at our desks as fast as possible so we can spend the rest of the hour on the playground.

I get home from school about three-thirty. Mother usually has a snack ready for me. Once I have finished eating, I take a short nap. This may seem strange to you. There is a good reason for it though. At six in the evening, I must be at the second school I attend. This is a *juku*, a private school that will help me prepare for the upcoming junior high school exams. Classes here go on until nine. Most of my friends attend these classes, too. Right now, I am taking only English and an extra math course. I have many problems with math. My mother is worried about this and has hired a private tutor to help me. He helps me every night for one hour.

My homework usually takes an hour and a half. I get to sleep about midnight. Truly, nowadays sleep is when I am happiest. I assure my mother that all is ready for the next day and fall asleep trying to think of things other than school.

Education in Japan

School Calendar

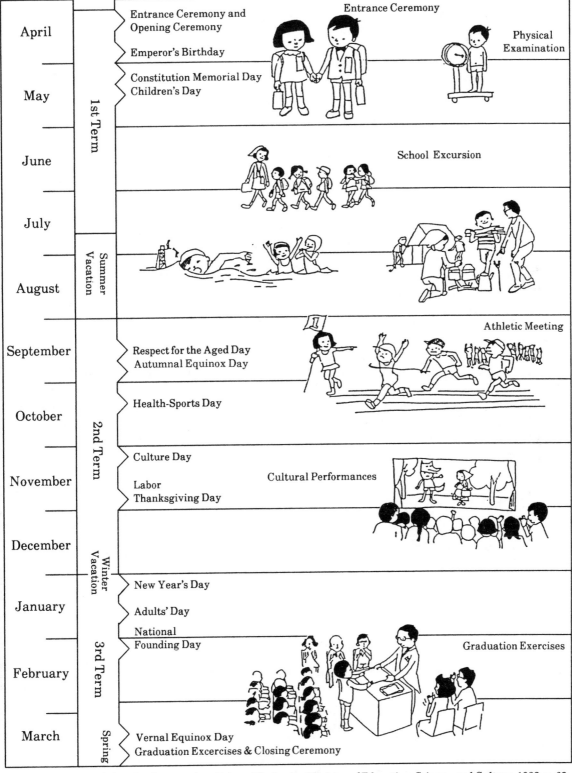

April	1st Term	Entrance Ceremony and Opening Ceremony

Entrance Ceremony and Opening Ceremony

Entrance Ceremony

Physical Examination

Emperor's Birthday

May — Constitution Memorial Day / Children's Day

June — School Excursion

July

August — Summer Vacation

September — Respect for the Aged Day / Autumnal Equinox Day — Athletic Meeting

October — Health-Sports Day

November — Culture Day / Labor Thanksgiving Day — Cultural Performances

2nd Term

December — Winter Vacation

January — New Year's Day / Adults' Day / National Founding Day

February — 3rd Term — Graduation Exercises

March — Spring — Vernal Equinox Day / Graduation Excercises & Closing Ceremony

Education in Japan, A Graphic Presentation. Tokyo: Monbusho, Ministry of Education, Science, and Culture, 1982, p. 69. p. 69.

Education in Japan

Japan's School System

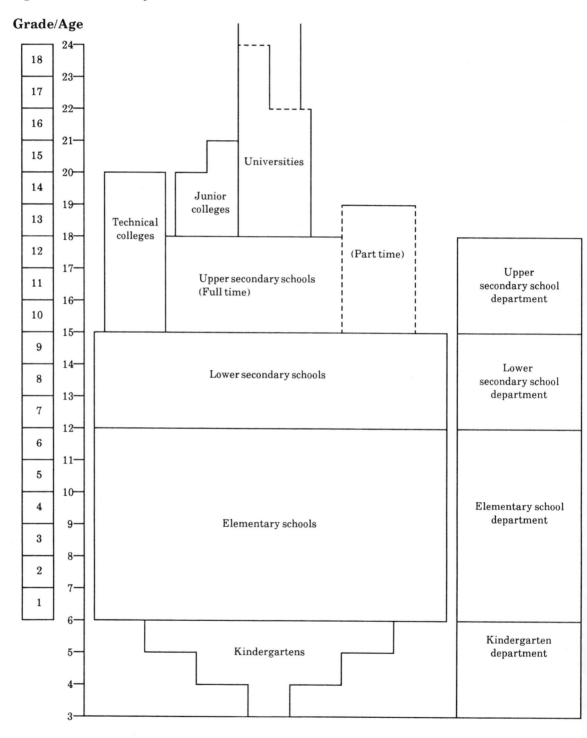

Source: adapted from *Statistical Handbook of Japan 1986*, pp. 129-130.

The huge success of Japan's economy is a major topic in today's business and political circles in the United States and all over the world. The relationship of the yen to the dollar has wide-ranging effects on the markets in London, Brussels, Bonn, and Taiwan. This was not the case prior to this century when Japan was isolated and self-sufficient. Farming and fishing were important since rice and fish provided the main ingredients for their diet. Most people were engaged in agriculture; tenant farmers were dependent on wealthy landowners for their livelihood.

Farming

Farming is still an important part of the Japanese economy. During the land reforms that followed World War II, large-acreage holdings were broken up and distributed to the farmers who actually tilled the land. Only 15 percent of the total land area of Japan can be cultivated. Despite this limitation, Japan produces 70 percent of its own food. Farms are small; in fact, the average is only 2.4 acres. Compare that to the average-sized Wisconsin farm of 198 acres! The major crop is rice, occupying 50 percent of the farmland. A new interest in dairying and stock breeding is emerging to meet increased demands for meat and dairy products, especially cheese. As in Wisconsin, the number of people engaged in farming has decreased as technology has replaced human labor with machine labor.

Fishing

Even though Western influences such as fast-food chains are changing Japan's eating habits, fish is still an important part of the daily Japanese diet. Japan once had the world's largest fishing industry, but setbacks have occurred because of international pressure to reduce distant-water fishing by Japanese fleets. Local consumption still demands a large catch, and efforts have been made to develop the freshwater fishing industry, "fish-farming" rainbow trout and eels. Aquaculture is encouraged in less-polluted coastal areas so that shrimp, oysters, and scallops can be raised and harvested there.

Manufacturing

Manufacturing plays a dominant role in Japan's economy, employing 25 percent of the labor force and accounting for 30 percent of its gross national product (GNP). Because of a growing export trade and domestic investment to sustain production for that trade, Japan's industrial output expanded by over 11 percent in 1984 and by almost five percent in 1985. For several years the iron and steel industry played an important role in Japan's economic growth, but the oil crisis of the 1970s brought about significant changes in the manufacturing makeup, forcing a new and wider base of production. Consequently, today Japan is strong not only in iron, steel, and automobile production, but has become a world leader in the electronics and chemical industries. The government's policies encouraging less dependence on foreign imports have led to controversy with its trading partners, and this continues to be a topic of great concern within Japan and throughout the rest of the world.

Economics

*Comparison of Economic Data for Japan and the United States**

	Japan	United States
GNP – 1985**	1.328 trillion dollars	3.947 trillion dollars
Percentage of total world GNP	10%	22%
GNP per capita – 1985**	$11,300	$16,690
Autos manufactured – 1984	7,073,000	7,773,000
Labor unions – 1984	Primarily company-based membership—29% of labor force	Primarily industry-based membership—less than 24% of labor force
Manufacturing wage rates 1984	$6.05 per hour	$9.17 per hour
Unemployment – 1985 [1]	2.6% of labor force	7% of labor force
Hours per average work week	37.3	40.2
Exports – 1985	$175.9 billion	$213.1 billion
Imports – 1985	$130.5 billion	$361.6 billion
Percentage of population of working age (15-65) in		
Agriculture	11%	4%
Industry	34%	31%
Service	55%	66%

*Except where indicated, the source for this data is the Joint Council of Economic Education.

***World Development Report, 1987*, published for the *World Book* by the Oxford University Press, 1987.

[1]Because of differences in collection, these may not be strictly comparable.

Economics

Comparison of Prices in Japan and Wisconsin

The price for one gallon of gas (February 1988)
510.975 yen = $3.93

Monthly middle-class income for university graduates in Japan (1986)*

Age	Salary[†]	
22	144,759 yen =	$1,113.53
25	164,012 yen =	$1,261.63
45	402,710 yen =	$3,097.76
50	455,893 yen =	$3,506.86

Price of beef steak‡

130 grams @ 3,000 yen = $23.07
150 grams @ 4,000 yen = $30.76
180 grams @ 5,000 yen = $38.46

Price of items at McDonalds (January 1988)

Regular Hamburger	210 yen	= $1.62
Big Mac	290	= 2.23
Cheeseburger	240	= 1.84
Double Burger	300	= 2.30
Double Cheeseburger	350	= 2.69
Small French Fries	120	= .92
Large French Fries	220	= 1.69
9-Piece Chicken McNuggets	200	= 1.53
Shake	220	= 1.69
Coffee	160	= 1.23

Source: Ministry of Labor
*Tax is excluded
[†]130 yen = $1.00 (1988)
‡454 grams = 1 pound

Economics

Products and Resources Map of Japan

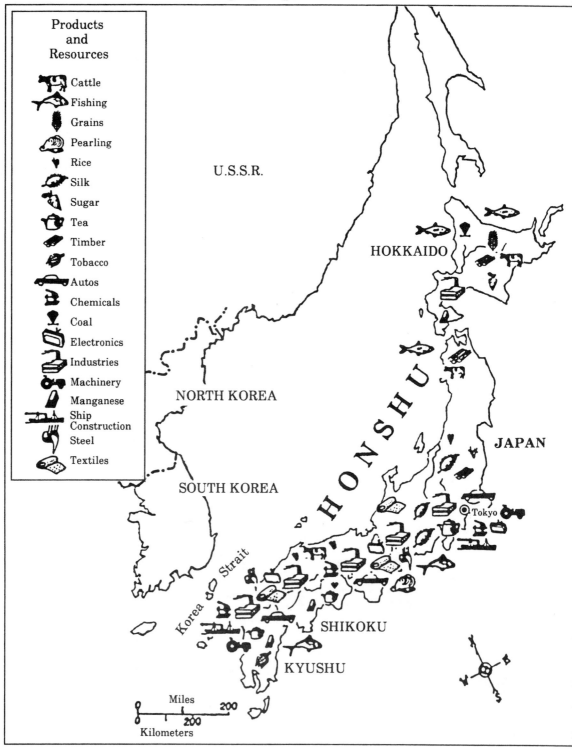

Source: Joint Council on Economic Education. *Teaching About the Japanese*, 1986, p. 27.

Products and Resources Map of Wisconsin

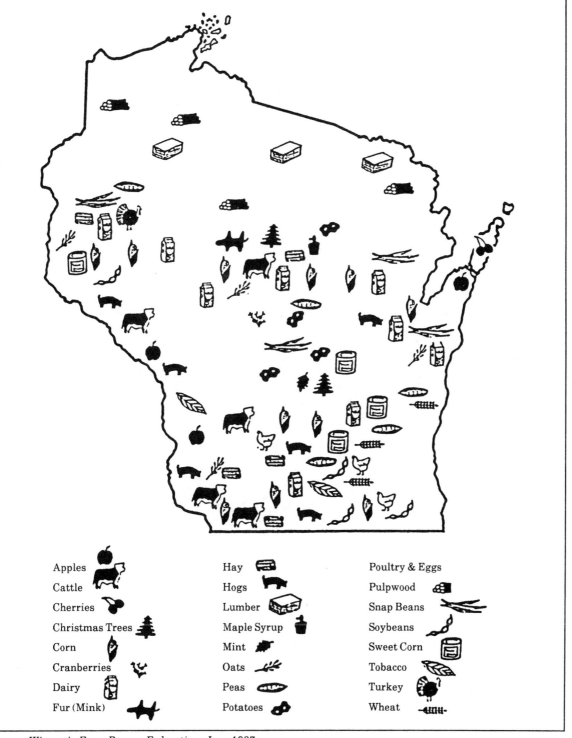

Apples	Hay	Poultry & Eggs	
Cattle	Hogs	Pulpwood	
Cherries	Lumber	Snap Beans	
Christmas Trees	Maple Syrup	Soybeans	
Corn	Mint	Sweet Corn	
Cranberries	Oats	Tobacco	
Dairy	Peas	Turkey	
Fur (Mink)	Potatoes	Wheat	

Source: Wisconsin Farm Bureau Federation. June 1987.

Economics

Japanese-Owned Firms in Wisconsin

Company	Wisconsin Location	Product	Number of Employees	Parent Company
IKE International Corp.	Stanley	hardwood, veneer and plywood	not available	Ikeuchi Industrial Corp., Hokkaido
Keihin Seki USA, Inc.	West Allis	internal combustion engines	3	Keihin Seiki Mfg. Co, Ltd., Tokyo
Kikkoman Foods Inc.	Walworth	pickles, sauces, and salad dressings	90	Kikkoman Corp., Noda Chiba
PMP Fermentation	Milwaukee	wines, brandy, and brandy spirits	not available	Fujisawa Pharmaceutical Co., Ltd., Osaka
Yusen Air and Sea Service Intl.	Oak Creek	freight forwarding	4	Yusen Air and Sea Chuo-Ku, Tokyo

Source: This information was compiled by the Wisconsin Department of Development and appeared in an article, "Foreign Firms Buy American," by Judy Wenzel in *The Milwaukee Journal*.

Economics

Foreign-Owned Wisconsin Companies (in whole or part)

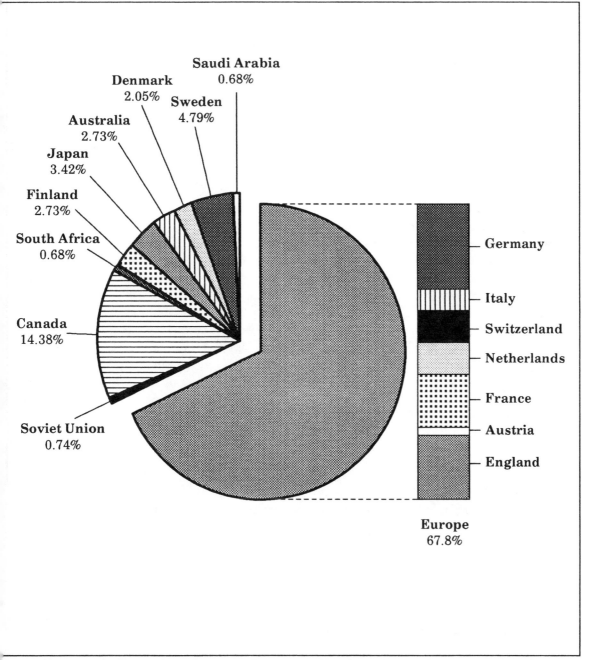

Saudi Arabia
0.68%

Denmark
2.05%

Sweden
4.79%

Australia
2.73%

Japan
3.42%

Finland
2.73%

South Africa
0.68%

Canada
14.38%

Soviet Union
0.74%

Germany

Italy

Switzerland

Netherlands

France

Austria

England

Europe
67.8%

Source: "Companies by Country Origin," Wisconsin Department of Development. November, 1986.

Energy, Transportation, and Pollution

Energy

A highly productive, technical, and industrial country such as Japan must be especially concerned with its supply of and demand for energy. Since the oil crisis of the early 1970s, when Japan's oil dependency was quite high, the country has been working to decrease its dependency on a single source of imported energy. The industrial sector has reduced somewhat the total amount of energy it uses, and is swinging away from oil toward nuclear power and coal.

In addition to efforts to decrease consumption, other efforts have been made to accommodate future energy needs. Strict laws for fuel emission standards on automobiles have been enacted. Subsidies for improved public transportation have helped reduce private car travel. Research continues for replacement of nonrenewable resources such as coal, oil, and natural gas. This includes the effort for development of geothermal, solar, and coal liquefaction technologies. Since Japan is continuing nuclear development, they have signed long-term agreements with suppliers of uranium.

Despite the problems involved—high costs, low availability of earthquake-free sites, and the length of time it takes to prepare and build plants—Japan's nuclear power supply is expected to meet about 16 percent of the country's energy needs by the year 2000. The Japanese were among the first in the world to witness the dangers of atomic radiation, but protests against the development of nuclear energy have been minimal.

Before World War II, coal had been a major source of energy in Japan; large coal fields existed in Joban (north of Tokyo), Hokkaido, and in northwestern areas of Kyushu. Increasing demands for energy combined with diminishing coal supplies, forced Japan to turn to petroleum. Today coal is seen as a viable substitute for oil and Japan imports coal in ultra-large bulk carriers. Although the increased use of coal will undoubtedly cause pollution problems, Japan has become the largest importer of coal in the world.

Transportation

Japan has one of the world's fastest and most efficient mass transit systems. Railroads were first introduced in 1872 and now link all major cities and towns. Japan's railroads carried 18 billion passengers in 1980—a world record. Rush-hour trains usually are jammed to overcapacity, and at some stations people are hired to push passengers into crowded rail cars.

Railways

Until recently most railroads were nationally owned and operated by Japanese National Railways. Now privately owned companies direct rail traffic. Japan's rail system is known for speed and efficiency; several super-express lines have "bullet" trains (*shinkansen*) that travel up to 130 miles per hour. New bullet railways are under construction, and eventually they will link Tokyo with all parts of the country.

As part of this effort, a 33.5-mile-long underwater tunnel has been built between the main island of Honshu and the northern island of Hokkaido. It has taken 42 years to plan and construct the Seikan Tunnel, completed in early 1988 and presently the world's newest and longest rail tunnel. It reduces travel time from Tokyo to Hokkaido to seven hours and 40 minutes. The Tappi rail station, located 640 feet below the surface of the sea, serves as an emergency center in the event of an accident in the tunnel.

Japan is developing rail systems powered by linear motors, in which cars will "float" over tracks on a magnetic field. Experimental prototypes have achieved speeds of 310 miles per hour. In addition, Japan is providing Amtrak with technical help in renovating railroads in the United States.

Motor Vehicles

Motor vehicles have come into wide use in the last two decades and most freight in Japan is now moved by truck. Most major roads are paved, and a national network of expressways (like America's interstate system) is under construction.

About two-thirds of all Japanese households own a car. The minimum age for licensed automobile drivers is 18, 16 for drivers of motorcycles. To register a car, prospective drivers must show proof that they have a place to park it, due to limited availability of land. Gasoline, refined from imported oil, is about $4.00 per gallon, one reason most Japanese cars are designed for fuel efficiency. Families living in cities use their cars mostly for weekend recreation. In rural areas, the car is often the most convenient way to travel from place to place and, as in the United States, is vital for daily life.

Air Travel

Most major Japanese cities are linked by air service, which has grown in importance in recent years. Japanese airlines carried 40.9 million passengers in 1980, ranking Japan third in the world in air transport, after the United States and the U.S.S.R.

Japan has over 1,000 ports along its coastline, and maritime shipping is an important means of moving bulk cargo. Most basic industries—iron and steel, chemical, cement, petroleum—make use of water transport. Much freight is containerized for rapid connection to rail and truck services. Ferries link virtually all of Japan's small offshore islands with the main islands.

Pollution

Given Japan's limited land area and large population it is no surprise that pollution is a major problem. In Wisconsin, water and air pollution cause public concern and high costs. Japan has similar concerns, but on a larger scale. The growth of industrial pollution was so great in the 25 years following World War II that it was said Japan was on the verge of poisoning itself. In addition, the increasing population and the ever-escalating standard of living have contributed significantly to pollution.

On the eastern coast of Japan, where industrial cities are congregated, the air has been heavy with sulfur dioxides. The number of privately owned cars in Japan more than tripled between 1970 and 1984. Damage to vegetation, buildings, and human health led to the passage of the 1968 Air Pollution Act. Alternate fuels, desulphurization of gases, taller chimneys, and strict exhaust emissions controls are some of the preventative measures taken since then.

In Wisconsin, an agriculture- and recreation-based state, one of the primary concerns is water quality and the problem of agricultural runoff into lakes and streams. The

Wisconsin Department of Natural Resources devotes much time and energy to monitoring non-point sources of pollutants which infect groundwater. In fact, the state's water pollution control budget for 1985-86 increased to more than $11 million. Clean water is of tremendous importance to Japan also, since the country depends on clean water for rice irrigation and uncontaminated oceans for the fishing industry. Environmental pollution control laws have been controversial in Japan's industrial circles. Despite the high costs of enforcement, partial success has been achieved, as witnessed by the revival of fishing in Tokyo Bay during the last few years.

Solid waste pollution can be tied directly to an increased standard of living, for as a society grows in affluence, it discards more items—refrigerators, cars, plastics, furniture. One way Japan disposes of solid wastes is by burning. This is a convenient method, but unfortunately adds to the level of air pollution. Another unsatisfactory method of disposal is ocean dumping. Barges carry urban refuse to dump far offshore in the Pacific Ocean. Land reclamation through landfill is perhaps the most useful strategy, and, in this, Japan's efforts have been successful. New land has been created for industry, recreation, and housing.

Energy, Transportation, and Pollution

Sources of Pollution

Air Pollution

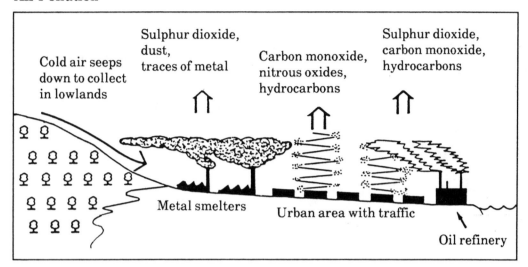

Water Pollution

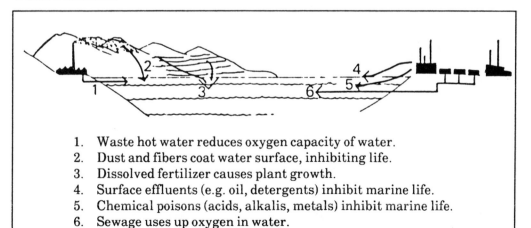

1. Waste hot water reduces oxygen capacity of water.
2. Dust and fibers coat water surface, inhibiting life.
3. Dissolved fertilizer causes plant growth.
4. Surface effluents (e.g. oil, detergents) inhibit marine life.
5. Chemical poisons (acids, alkalis, metals) inhibit marine life.
6. Sewage uses up oxygen in water.

Source: MacDonald, Donald. *A Geography of Modern Japan*, 1985, pp. 105-106.

References

Japan, A Pocket Guide. Foreign Press Center, 1986.

Japan. Oklahoma Department of Education, 1983.

MacDonald, Donald. *A Geography of Modern Japan.* Paul Norbury Publications, 1985.

Noh, Toshio and John C. Kimura. *Japan: A Regional Geography of an Island Nation.* Teikoku-Shoin Co., Ltd., 1983.

Sexton, Bill and Bonnie. "Newest Joy for Rail Buffs: World's Deepest Station." *Newsday*, March 13, 1988.

Statistical Handbook of Japan. Statistics Bureau, Management and Coordination Agency, 1986.

Tokyo: International Society for Educational Information, 1986.

What I Want to Know About Japan. Third ed. Japan Information Center, 1983.

Activities: Government, Education, and Society

6

The Elementary School in Japan and Wisconsin
Japanese and American Workers: Work Values
Comparative Standards of Living
Japanese Impact on U.S. Hometown Markets
Scarcity: Natural Resources

The Elementary School in Japan and Wisconsin

Activity 1: Elementary Level, 3-6

These are sample activities, or examplars, only. They can be used as described or re-modeled to suit local needs. They also may suggest ideas for additional learning experiences for elementary students.

Objectives

- To observe the Japanese school day
- To compare and contrast the typical Japanese school day with the student's own
- To recognize and make inferences about how each type of schooling is both a product of and a contributor to the community
- To draw conclusions about the unique characteristics of Japanese and Wisconsin schooling

Materials

- "Our School." *The Video Letter from Japan.* The Asia Society, 1982
- Activity Sheet 1: Questions for Discussion
- Activity Sheet 2: If I Went to School in Japan
- Activity Sheet 3: Discussion of the School Year

Suggested Procedures

1. Prepare for viewing the film by discussing informally some things we take for granted in our schools: summer vacation, recess, physical education, grading system, passing to the next level. Discuss differences in types of schools, in what schools do, in where money comes from for school. Students should watch for things that are different from their school as they view the film.
2. View film together.
3. Discuss differences—record on chalkboard. Students might give these answers: wearing uniforms, kindergarten not a part of elementary school, reception of first graders, older students help younger children, changing shoes, morning assembly.
4. Using Questions for Discussion, Activity Sheet 1, help class draw inferences about differences between U.S. and Japanese communities based on some of their observations.
5. Students can write their thoughts about going to school in Japan on Activity Sheet 2.
6. Share written paragraphs with class.
7. Activity Sheet 3: Discussion of the School Year will permit students to draw inferences from an important difference between the two cultures. Older elementary students might enjoy forming debate teams to discuss whether one culture takes schooling more seriously than the other. Encourage them to think broadly about the issues and to provide evidence for their opinions.

Follow-Up Activities

1. Design a teaching-learning plan and time schedule for a typical Japanese school day and let children help implement it, assign tasks, and so forth.
2. Use the Japanese exercises with the class on a regular basis. A cassette tape and instruction sheet are available from the East Asia Center, University of Wisconsin-Madison, 1440 Van Hise Hall, Madison WI 53706.

Additional Easy Activities

1. Using a chart, contrast a year in the life of a Japanese student with a year in the life of a Wisconsin student. After you decide on the age, sex, and urban or rural environments of the students, contrast their levels of attendance at school, studying at home, participation in community activities, after-school jobs, plans to go on vacation, television viewing habits, reading (outside of school assignments), music lessons, favorite foods. If possible, interview a visiting student from Japan for an authentic viewpoint.
2. You are a Japanese elementary student visiting the United States for the first time. After staying with relatives in California for the first two days, you set off on a whirlwind trip to see the United States in two weeks. Where would you like to visit and what would you like to eat? How would you react to visiting an American school? What are your impressions of Glacier Park, Lake Superior, fishing on a northern Wisconsin lake? Record your impressions in a journal.

The Elementary School in Japan and Wisconsin

Questions for Discussion

1. In the film, you saw older students helping the younger children. Do you think this is a good idea? Why? Why not?

2. Not only do school children take time for morning exercises, but so do all workers in Japan. Why do you think they do this? (People might be more physically fit. People work better if they exercise first. Environments are cool, and it is a way to warm up.) Can you list some other reasons?

3. Why do Japanese schools give "credit" for extracurricular activities?

4. Let's look at the activities that emphasize cooperation: cleaning the school together, field trips, class meetings, group sporting events. This is an important idea in Japanese schools. What might this tell us about Japanese families and Japanese communities?

5. How much leisure time would a Japanese student have during a typical day? How is this similar to or different from a typical day for a Wisconsin student of the same age?

The Elementary School in Japan and Wisconsin

If I Went to School in Japan

Directions: Write a reaction paragraph for each of the following ideas. Include your thoughts about schedule, homework, extracurricular activities, possible transportation problems, foreign language classes, and even lunch.

A. What I'd Like About Going to School in Japan:

B. What I Wouldn't Like About Going to School in Japan:

115

The Elementary School in Japan and Wisconsin

Discussion of the School Year

School terms in Japan begin in April, September, and January; school is also held on Saturday, and special events are held on Sundays so the whole family can attend. The total number of days per year is 240.

1. How long is the school year in Wisconsin? When are school terms and activities held?

2. What do these facts tell us about how important schooling is in Japan?

3. What do these facts tell us about how important schooling is in the United States?

Japanese and American Workers: Work Values

Activity 2: Junior/Senior High Level

This activity was adapted from *Teaching About the Japanese Economy*, Joint Council on Economic Education, 1986, New York, NY 10016, pp. 46-47. Reprinted with permission.

These are sample activities, or examplars, only. They can be used as described or remodeled to suit local needs. They also may suggest ideas for additional learning experiences for junior and senior high school students.

Objectives

- To demonstrate an understanding of the major differences in American and Japanese work attitudes
- To identify some cultural factors that affect work attitudes in Japan and the United States

Materials

- Activity Sheet 1: A Comparison of Workers
- Activity Sheet 2: Questions for Discussion

Suggested Procedures

1. Either hand out or place on the board the data from the article in *U.S. News and World Report*, September 2, 1985, which compares American and Japanese workers. The author of the article asked ten leading scholars of the American and Japanese workplace to rate both countries' workers.
2. Ask the students for their reactions to the ratings. It is important that they realize the relationship between the culture and the workplace. Discussion should focus on the following question: "What is it about American/Japanese cultures that causes each country's workers to demonstrate a particular work trait?"
3. Ask the students to write two short paragraphs contrasting American and Japanese workers, citing reasons for the differences in American and Japanese attitudes toward work.

Japanese and American Workers: Work Values

Background Information: Work

Although they are among the world's most productive workers, Americans and Japanese often have quite different perceptions of work. The purpose of this lesson is to assist students in comparing and contrasting Japanese and American attitudes toward work.

Japan's unemployment rate is 2.6 percent (1985), about one-third of that of the United States. The major reason for this difference is that large Japanese companies have "lifetime employment" systems. Japanese worker absenteeism rates are half that of U.S. workers.

The average Japanese person works 2,116 hours a year, about two months more than the 1,883 annual hours of a U.S. worker. Most Japanese arrive early, routinely work overtime, and work on Saturdays.

For additional reference reading, *The Japanese* by Edwin Reischauer and *The Shadows of the Rising Sun* by Jared Taylor are excellent books that contain useful background to and information on cultural attitudes and work.

Japanese and American Workers: Work Values

A Comparison of Workers

United States	Characteristic	Japan
	Concern for Quality Japanese workers possess a fervent desire to do the job well. They pay great attention to detail. Many Americans just want to finish the job.	X
X	**Initiative** On an individual level, Americans are willing to demonstrate initiative. They are concerned with who gets credit for exceptional work.	
	Hard Work The work ethic is strong in both countries, but the experts give the Japanese a slight edge because they routinely put in extra hours. Their company is the central focus of their lives.	X
	Honesty Because of strong identification with their company, Japanese are less likely to steal office supplies or cheat on time cards and expense accounts.	X
X	**Ambition** American's individualistic culture encourages workers to strive to get ahead. Japanese, though ambitious, try not to stand out, especially early in their careers.	
	Loyalty The average Japanese worker expects to spend an entire career at one firm. Companies, in turn, take a paternalistic interest in employees.	X
	Basic Skills Japan's schools produce graduates with good basic skills. Japanese learn discipline and good work habits that they transfer to the job.	X
X	**Advanced Skills** A close call. Workers in both nations are highly educated, but the U.S. has more college graduates and white-collar professionals.	
	Reliability Japanese are reluctant to show up late or call in sick, largely because they don't want to let down their bosses and co-workers. Many skip part of their vacations.	X
	Cooperativeness Japanese subordinate individual concerns to group needs. This fosters a spirit of togetherness that is especially effective on the assembly line.	X

Source: *U.S. News and World Report,* September 2, 1985, p. 41.

Japanese and American Workers: Work Values

Questions for Discussion

1. How are cultures similar to and different from one another?

2. How do American values and views about work differ from those of other cultures?

3. What economic and political challenges are likely to face the United States in the twenty-first century?

Comparative Standards of Living

Activity 3: High School Level

This activity is used with permission of the authors: Betty Cowley and Jerry D. Johnson. *Japan in American Economics: Teaching Strategies and Resources,* 1987, pp. 61-68. This activity was designed to accompany *Teaching About Japanese Economy,* published by the Joint Council on Economic Education, 1986.

These are sample activities, or examplars, only. They can be used as described or remodeled to suit local needs. They also may suggest ideas for additional economic experiences for high school students.

Objectives

- To read and correctly interpret given tables
- To differentiate between national income and per capita income
- To differentiate between quantity and quality in GNP and standards of living
- To compare, through an analysis of data, the changes of living between charted cities

Materials

- Activity Sheet 1: Big Mac Index
- Activity Sheet 2: Study Guide: Comparative Buying Power
- Overhead transparency of Big Mac Index (for discussion)
- Standard of Living Indicators, Activity Sheet 3.
- Graph paper and straightedge for each student
- Measuring tape, string, or rope
- Measurement of own bedroom (optional)
- Activity Sheet 4: Questions for Discussion

Suggested Procedures

1. Explain or review the concept of standard of living and problems in making comparisons.
2. Hand out Big Mac Index (Activity Sheet 1) and Study Guide (Activity Sheet 2). Have students complete the exercise and discuss their answers. A discussion of why Japan's standard of living is increasing while that of other nations is decreasing may be useful.
3. Distribute Standard of Living Indicators, Activity Sheet 3, then study and discuss the table and the graph using Activity Sheet 4: Questions for Discussion.
4. Distribute graph paper with the following assignment. Using each square of the graph paper as one square foot, the student is to design an apartment floor plan with kitchen, bath, living, and sleeping rooms or areas, keeping total floor space to 800 square feet. (If students did bring in measurements of their own rooms, it might be interesting to ask them to place their room in the floor plan before adding the other rooms.)

5. Select a plan or two from the class and mark off the appropriate space in the classroom. (You may use standing students, rope, or string as walls.)
6. Discuss how family life in Japan must be different than life in U.S., noting areas such as privacy; ownership and storage of possessions; multi-use furniture and rooms; entertaining, cooking, and study facilities.
7. Students can update the statistics presented in the activities by referring to the *World Almanac 1990*, *Facts on File*, and other standard materials. Ask them to find current data for those categories listed in the charts and graphs, and to make comparisons with the historical data presented. Discuss how changes in the statistics might affect their conclusions and reasoning in the activities.

Comparative Standards of Living

Background Information: Economics

Many people still think of Japan as an impoverished, backward "third world" nation where most workers are overworked, underpaid, and living under intolerable conditions. This is not accurate. In fact, projections show that by the year 2000 Japan's per capita income will be greater than that of the United States. Japan is a modern industrial nation whose people are reaping the benefits of its wealth.

An important key to understanding comparative standards of living is knowing that local factors, such as wages, taxes, and inflation rates make direct comparisons of prices useless. Therefore, analysis of the purchasing power of workers is perhaps the most useful tool for comparison. The Big Mac Index (see next page) comparison by Howard Banks (from *Forbes*, July 2, 1984, pp. 110-111) makes analysis of the standard of living differentials easily understood and enjoyable.

At the same time, it must be generally recognized that quantity does not always mean quality. In Japan this discrepancy is demonstrated by its housing limitations. Japan is very crowded with 316 people per square kilometer, compared to China with 106 per square kilometer, West Germany with 247 per square kilometer, and the U.S. with 25 per square kilometer. Because of this crowding, Japan's is some of the most expensive real estate in the world, with Tokyo lots selling for $18,000 per square meter. Therefore, building costs are exceptionally high and will continue to soar, limiting the availability of housing. As a result, the Japanese quality of living suffers: the average Japanese family lives in a residence with four rooms and a total area of 800 square feet.

Comparative Standards of Living

The Big Mac Index

Earning a Big Mac

The Big Mac Index discloses that Chicago bus drivers had to work 4 minutes longer in 1984 than in 1979 to pay for the same meal. They did better than their French counterparts, who had to drive 40 minutes more. Japanese drivers, on the other hand, needed to drive 24 minutes less.

Hours worked to buy Big Macs, small fries, and regular cokes for 4.

2:30

2:00

1979

1984

1:30

1:00

0:30

Chicago   Tokyo   Paris   Düsseldorf   London

Source: *Forbes,* July 2, 1984. Forbes Inc., 1984. Adapted with permission.

Comparative Standard of Living

Study Guide: Comparative Buying Power

Directions: The Big Mac Index shows a comparison of the changing standard of living among various countries. For all the differences in wages, taxes, inflation, and culture, an hour of work is roughly comparable throughout the entire industrial world. This chart shows the number of hours a bus driver needed to work to earn enough to buy Big Macs, small fries, and medium Cokes for a family of four. Read the chart carefully and answer the following questions.

1. Approximately how many hours did a Chicago bus driver have to work to earn the cost of the Big Mac meal in 1979?

2. How many hours did a London driver have to work to earn the cost of the meal in 1984?

3. Between 1979 and 1984, which city's bus drivers saw the greatest increase in the number of hours they had to work to earn the cost of the meal?

   How much of an increase, in hours and/or minutes, did bus drivers in that city have to work to earn the meal's cost?

4. In which city during this period did hours of work required to purchase the meal increase the least?

   How much of an increase was that?

5. Where did the number of hours of work needed to earn the meal actually drop during this period?

   By how many hours and/or minutes?

6. According to this index, which country (as represented by its sample city) had the highest standard of living in 1979? In 1984?

7. According to this index, which country had the poorest standard of living in 1979? In 1984?

8. What are some reasons that account for differences in standards of living found around the world?

Comparative Standards of Living

Standard of Living Indicators

Percentage of Japanese Households Owning Selected Consumer Goods, 1970-1980

Item	Ownership Rate %	
	1970	1980
Refrigerators	89.1	99.1
Washing Machines	91.4	98.8
Color TV	26.3	98.2
Vacuum Cleaners	68.3	95.8
Cameras	64.1	82.9
Passenger Cars	22.1	57.2
Stereos	31.2	57.1
Air Conditioners	5.9	39.2

Source: *Perspectives on Japan: A Guide for Teachers* (Bulletin No. 68), National Council for the Social Studies.

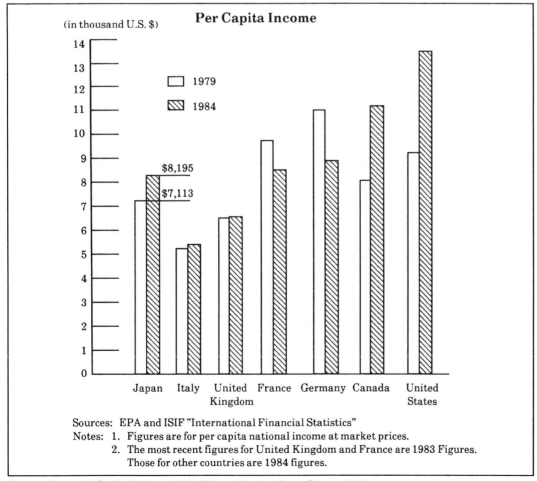

Per Capita Income

(in thousand U.S. $)

1979
1984

$8,195
$7,113

Japan · Italy · United Kingdom · France · Germany · Canada · United States

Sources: EPA and ISIF "International Financial Statistics"
Notes: 1. Figures are for per capita national income at market prices.
2. The most recent figures for United Kingdom and France are 1983 Figures. Those for other countries are 1984 figures.

Source: *Economic Outlook, Japan 1986*. Tokyo: Foreign Press Center, 1986.

Comparative Standards of Living

Questions for Discussion

1. How have patterns of consumption in the West influenced Japan?

2. What major changes in consumption of goods have taken place in Japan over the years?

3. How have the consumer habits of Japanese and Americans changed during the twentieth century? How has each society influenced the other?

4. What can we conclude about the relationship between United States trade policies with Japan and our national economic well-being?

Japanese Impact on U.S. Hometown Markets

Activity 4: High School Level

This activity is used with permission of the authors: Betty Cowley and Jerry D. Johnson. *Japan in American Economics: Teaching Strategies and Resources*, 1987, pp. 33-37. This activity was designed to accompany *Teaching About Japanese Economy*, published by the Joint Council on Economic Education, 1986.

These are sample activities, or examplars, only. They can be used as described or re-modeled to suit local needs. They also may suggest ideas for additional learning experiences for high school students.

Objectives

● To list specific Japanese products that directly compete with local or area businesses'
● To explain how Japanese competition has direct effects on the local community
● To become aware of the impact of Japanese imports and exports on U.S. hometown markets

Materials

● Activity Sheet 1: Product Manufacturers List
● Activity Sheet 2: Questions for Discussion
● Teacher-compiled address list of area businesses and industries selling imports, and of businesses and industries in direct competition for the imports' markets.
● Activity sheets 3 and 4: Interview Questions

Suggested Procedures

1. The teacher and class will become familiar with sources of products by reviewing Activity Sheet 1: Product Manufacturers List.
2. Each student or group of students should be given a particular area businessperson or factory executive representative to interview by phone or in person.
3. Each student reports interview findings to class while a record of information (product inroads) is listed on board.
4. Finally, the class analyzes the effects of Japanese imports on local businesses.

Follow-up Activity

Invite a speaker from an important or interesting local business to visit class and discuss the local impact of Japanese competition.

Additional Easy Activities

1. Collect pictures of Japanese products, and mount these on heavy paper. Find out the approximate dollar price of each by checking newspaper advertisements. Using the current value of the yen, figure out the price of each item. Chart the comparative

prices; follow up with a discussion on why American consumers choose one product over another.

2. Prepare graph contrasting ownership of American and Japanese products in the homes of students and of teachers. How many or what percent own American versus Japanese microwaves, hairdryers, computers, cars, or radios? What are the owners' attitudes about product reliability, prices, and design?

3. After discussing Japanese–U.S. trade and business relations in class, plan an advertising campaign. Show how a particular product might be sold successfully in the Japanese market if it is sold by Americans. Discuss how cultural factors might help or hinder sales. Examples of products might include professional football, cake mix, golf carts, home heating furnaces, designer bubble bath.

Japanese Impact on U.S. Hometown Markets

Product Manufacturers List

Some Japanese products and services sold in the United States

Automobiles
Datsun
Honda
Toyota
Mazda
Subaru
Nissan
Isuzu

Electronic Equipment
Toshiba
Panasonic
Sony
Quasar
Sanyo
Hitachi

Steel
Nippon Steel

Tires
Bridgestone

Airlines
Japan Air Lines (JAL)
All Nippon Airways (ANA)

Cameras
Nikon
Canon
Minolta
Pentax
Konica

Film
Fuji

Motorcycles
Suzuki
Kawasaki
Yamaha

Tableware
Noritake China
Mikasa Glassware

Watches
Casio
Seiko

Heavy Equipment
Komatsu

Source: This list is adapted from the "Partial List of Japanese Goods and Services..." in *Teaching About the Japanese Economy*, Joint Council on Economic Education, 1986, p. 51.

Japanese Impact on U.S. Hometown Markets

Questions for Discussion

1. With what type of product(s) do the Japanese exert the greatest influence locally? Describe their influence and list reasons why this is so.

2. How does Japanese product intrusion affect local job markets? Are any of the imported products also produced locally? Do the import products businesses have Japanese salespeople, repairmen, managers, etc?

3. Where these products are concerned, is the Japanese influence growing, declining, or remaining constant?

4. Under what circumstances do you (or your family) purchase Japanese products? Why?

5. Describe experiences you (or your family) have had in getting Japanese products repaired, replaced, etc.? Is this situation improving, getting worse, etc.?

6. Did any of the products listed surprise you as being Japanese-made? Which? Why?

7. How have Japanese imports changed production locally? How have these changes been beneficial or detrimental?

8. How have imports changed retail sales? How have these changes been beneficial or detrimental?

9. What are some of the likely major impacts of Japanese competition on the local economy in five years? Ten years?

Japanese Impact on U.S. Hometown Markets

Suggested Interview Questions

Subject: Local Factory or Industry Affected by Japanese Competition

1. Name of company

2. Name of individual interviewed

3. Position of individual interviewed

4. Type of product(s) produced

5. Number of employees in local plant

6. Average wage/hour

7. What is the company's annual payroll?

8. What is the estimated amount of money invested into local economy by this company?

9. What is the size (market share) of local company in relationship to industry?

10. Describe the changing status of market share in recent years—is market share growing, declining or remaining constant?

11. Does the company have any Japanese competitor(s)? Who? What product(s) is (are) produced by the competitor(s)?

12. Where are these Japanese products produced? (Japan, the United States, or some other country?)

13. In what ways is the local company attempting to meet Japanese competition? Examples might include increasing or improving technology, quality control, just-in-time inventory management procedures, other measures to increase productivity, give-backs, expansion of shifts, and attitude changes.

Japanese Impact on U.S. Hometown Markets

Suggested Interview Questions

Subject: Local Retail Outlet That Sells Japanese Products

1. Name of retail store

2. Name of individual interviewed

3. Position of individual interviewed

4. Number of employees locally

5. Type of product(s) sold

6. Approximately when did the sale of Japanese imports become important to this business?

7. What change in market share has occurred since initial introduction of Japanese imports?

8. How has ordering, delivery, and service changed for the business due to imports?

9. What special benefits and problems have imports caused for the business?

10. What are typical consumer reactions to imports, including preferences expressed, common complaints, etc.?

11. What special benefits and problems have imports caused the consumer?

12. Compare quality of domestic and imported products

13. What are future prospects for continued sales of imports?

Japanese Impact on U.S. Hometown Markets

Study Guide

1. How might today's technological change have a similar impact on us as the Industrial Revolution did on people of the past?

2. What are some of the important and unique contributions of Asian nations to the rest of the world?

3. What issues and challenges does the United States face at the beginning of its third century? How are political institutions at the local, state, national, and international levels responding to these challenges?

4. How is your community an example of global interdependence?

Scarcity: Natural Resources

Activity 5: High School Level

This activity was adapted from *Teaching About the Japanese Economy*, copyright 1986, Joint Council on Economic Education, New York, NY 10016.

These are sample activities, or examplars, only. They can be used as described or re-modeled to suit local needs. They also may suggest ideas for additional natural resource experiences for high school students.

Objectives

- To discuss Japan's natural resources scarcity
- To describe how scarcity affects economic reasoning in Japan
- To explain the economic effects of scarcity on Japan
- To explain how scarcity in Japan affects international relationships
- To analyze the overall effects of scarcity on Japanese domestic and international life by classifying the degree of scarcity of natural and human resources

Materials

- Activity Sheet 1: Product and Resources Map of Japan
- Activity Sheet 2: A Lack of Resources
- Activity Sheet 3: Imports by Selected Countries
- Activity Sheet 4: Natural Resources: Import Dependency
- Activity Sheet 5: Japan's Resource Imports: Top Three Suppliers
- Activity Sheet 6: Japan's Imports by Commodity
- Activity Sheet 7: Japan's Food Demand and Supply
- Activity Sheet 8: Import of Foodstuffs by Country
- Activity Sheet 9: Questions for Discussion

Background

The essential natural resources necessary for production are scarce and the available supply of them is changing constantly. Countries have varying amounts of these resources. Japan is particularly dependent on trade because of an acute, limited supply of natural resources. Japan continues to increase its demand for resources necessary to supply the needs of an industrial economy and to sustain economic growth. Maintaining a stable volume of essential resources is an important activity for business and government in Japan. The constant pressure to secure resources bears on many economic decisions and adds an additional element of stress to Japanese society.

Suggested Procedures

1. Begin the lesson by having students discuss what is meant by natural resources. Remind them that natural resources are gifts of nature used to produce goods and services. Have students identify examples of natural resources that can be found in Japan. Explain that some resources are used up and some can be renewed either by themselves (such as trees) or by the efforts of caring and reasonable people (such as soil). Scarce resources are obtained by trading with other countries.

2. Give students Activity Sheet 1: Product and Resources Map of Japan, and have them follow the directions. Discuss: What resources appear to be scarce in Japan? (Coal, minerals, land, land for raising dairy cattle, and tea.) What resources appear to be plentiful? (Fish, forests, industry.) What must Japan do to get the scarce resources? (trade, build up production, renew depleted resources, develop alternative resources, conserve, limit growth, limit resource use).

3. Have students read A Lack of Resources, Activity Sheet 2, and list the named resources on the Scarcity Continuum Graph at the bottom of Activity Sheet 3. Let students make a general listing, for development in a following lesson.

4. Have students look at Activity Sheet 4: Natural Resources: Import Dependency and write a list of the 12 natural resources based on the degree of import dependency, from aluminum-nickel (100%) to zinc (64.2%). Ask them to rank Japan with other countries, following the directions on the sheet. (Overall, Japan is one of the most resource-dependent countries in the world.)

5. Have students copy the following list of products from the chalkboard: crude oil, coal, wood, iron ore, maize (feeding), copper, raw cotton, pulp, wool, natural rubber, sugar. Speculate on which countries would provide Japan with these goods. Give students Activity Sheet 5: Japan's Resource Imports: Top Three Suppliers, and compare this list with their guesses. Discuss the economic and/or political effects of more or less trade dependency. As a group activity, students could represent a country, look up its major exports in the *World Almanac*, and set up a "for sale" sign listing those products. Students could take turns representing Japan as a buyer. Looking at the top three suppliers, some students might calculate which country Japan is most dependent upon for resources.

6. Ask students to study Activity Sheet 6: Japan's Imports By Commodity and follow the directions on the sheet. Optional: Have students plot a graph for each product trend and write brief observations about each. The class might also discuss why these trends have occurred (shifts in production of goods with Japan attempting to become more technologically independent and labor intensive).

7. Activity Sheet 7: Japan's Food Demand and Supply illustrates how domestic consumption is calculated. (See note #2 for formula.) Students should compare demand for food and food supply by doing the activity outlined on the activity sheet. Ask students also to compare consumption of different foods (such as cereals vs. rice). Why does Japan restrict the import of products like rice and oranges? How do changes in consumption (less rice, more bread; or less fish, more meat) create scarcities? (Effects: undersupply, decrease in self-sufficiency, more imports, higher prices.)

8. Using Activity Sheet 8: Import of Foodstuffs by Country, students can work in groups that have been assigned two categories of foodstuffs. Have students follow the directions on the activity sheet. Appoint a recorder in each group, and have groups discuss their observations based on these recorded remarks.

Scarcity: Natural Resources

Products and Resources Map of Japan

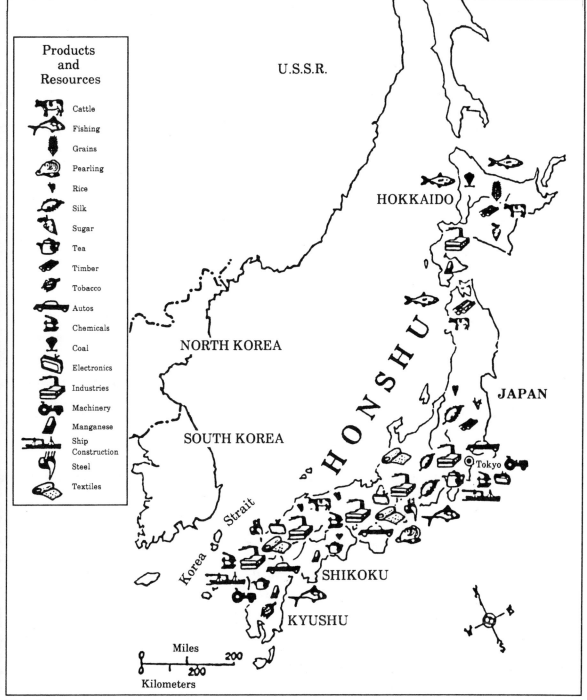

Directions

1. List each resource and mark the number of times it appears on the reference map.
2. Which resources appear to be scarce? Which are plentiful? (Mark the plentiful resources with a " + ," the scarce ones with a "-.")

Scarcity: Natural Resources

A Lack of Resources

Directions: Read the following article about Japan's resources. Study Activity Sheet 3: Industrial Imports by Selected Countries, and Activity Sheet 4: Natural Resources: Import Dependency.

Japan lacks natural resources and must import most of the raw materials necessary for industry. Since most of the land in Japan is unsuitable for farming, the Japanese must use intensive methods of production. For example, farmers give special and personalized attention to cultivating and harvesting. Special fertilizer, machinery, and irrigation are used. Despite careful farming methods, the Japanese must still import about 25 percent of their food.

One of the most plentiful food resources and a main source of protein in the Japanese diet is fish. Japan is located near seas where fish are abundant; its island geography, with long, indented coastlines, is ideal for the fishing industry. Japan's fishing industry is the world's largest —it accounts for one-sixth of the world's fish catch. Japan also has local fishing fleets comprised of hundreds of small boats, as well as a large oceangoing fleet of floating canneries. Freshwater fishing industries and aquaculture programs supply a wide variety of fish and seaweed.

Over two-thirds of Japan's land area is covered by trees, making it one of the world's most heavily forested nations. Cutting trees, however, is regulated strictly to conserve supplies of trees and to prevent soil erosion. Thus, Japan imports wood and wood products.

Japan produces some minerals (sulphur, copper, lead, zinc), but lacks other raw materials needed for industrial production. For example, iron and coal are necessary to make steel, but no iron-ore deposits exist in Japan, and coal is of limited quantity and poor quality. Most of the energy resources such as oil and natural gas are imported. Japan's efforts to develop alternative energy resources have not minimized its dependence on other countries for natural resources for industrial use. Japan's imports of these valuable, industrial resources are illustrated in the following table.

Scarcity: Natural Resources

Industrial Imports by Selected Countries in U.S. $ Millions (1982)

Importing Country	Iron Ore	Nonferrous Metals	Coal
Japan	3,629	2,570	5,787
U.S.A.	589	1,977	76
West Germany	1,058	1,012	765
France	382	501	1,438
Italy	418	235	1,339
United Kingdom	299	812	334
Canada	156	397	753
Netherlands	144	449	696
Australia	3	10	2

Source: OECD. *Statistics of Foreign Trade.*

Directions: Place major resources discussed in Activity Sheet 2 on the Scarcity Continuum Graph. What is a resource that Japan must import in large quantities? In small quantities?

Scarcity Continuum Graph

Very Scarce   Scarce   Least Scarce

141

Scarcity: Natural Resources

Natural Resources: Import Dependency (1982)

Resource	Degree of Import Dependency (%)				
	Japan	U.S.A.	West Germany	France	U.K.
Energy	83.5	12.3	52.1	76.1	−10.8
Coal	82.9	−16.9	−0.6	56.9	−3.9
Oil	89.8	32.9	94.7	98.3	−26.2
Natural Gas	91.4	4.1	65.4	74.5	24.6
Iron Ore	99.7	23.8	96.7	31.8	95.3
Copper	95.9	31.4	99.8	100.0	99.8
Lead	87.0	52.7	91.1	97.0	98.5
Zinc	64.2	58.8	71.3	86.0	94.4
Tin	98.3	99.8	100.0	100.0	59.6
Aluminum	100.0	79.9	100.0	−200.3	100.0
Nickel	100.0	96.9	100.0	100.0	100.0
Wood and Lumber	64.3	1.2	20.7	12.2	68.6

Directions: List Japan's resources below from most (100%) dependent to least (64.3%) dependency. Mark a "+" after each resource for which Japan is more dependent upon imports than other countries are, and a "−" if Japan is less dependent than other countries are.

Scarcity: Natural Resources

Japan's Resource Imports: Top Three Suppliers (1983)

Resource	Amount Imported (US$ millions)	Top Three Suppliers (%)					
		#1		#2		#3	
Crude Oil	40,063	Saudi Arabia	32.8	U.A.E.	15.9	Indonesia	14.5
Coal	4,877	Australia	45.6	U.S.A.	25.0	Canada	15.5
Wood	3,887	U.S.A.	30.4	Malaysia	29.4	Canada	11.0
Iron Ore	3,147	Australia	42.0	Brazil	22.8	India	12.9
Maize (Feeding)	1,572	U.S.A.	99.7	Argentina	0.3		—
Copper	1,475	Canada	23.0	Philippines	9.8		—
Raw Cotton	1,145	U.S.A.	47.3	U.S.S.R.	6.9	Egypt	6.3
Pulp	888	Canada	40.2	U.S.A.	33.0		—
Wool	560	Australia	66.0	New Zealand	14.9	South Africa	4.9
Natural Rubber	469	Thailand	64.7	Malaysia	23.1	Indonesia	10.3
Sugar	393	Thailand	31.2	Australia	26.5	Cuba	14.6

Source: Japan Tariff Association. *Foreign Trade Almanac*, 1984.

1. Which countries are Japan's major resource suppliers?

2. How would being a major resource supplier affect a country's diplomatic relations (political, economic, and military agreements) with Japan?

3. How would Japan's status as a major importer affect its relations with other countries?

Scarcity: Natural Resources

Japan's Imports by Commodity: 1968-1984 (U.S. $ Millions)

Commodity	1968	1973	1982	1983	1984
Foodstuffs	1,879	6,009	14,575	14,896	16,027
Textile Materials	952	2,188	2,327	2,077	2,484
Textiles	161	1,715	3,434	2,987	3,875
Metal Ores and Scrap	1,649	4,033	6,757	6,513	6,572
Iron Ore	834	1,652	3,630	3,147	3,199
Other Raw Materials	2,265	6,038	9,827	9,622	10,469
Mineral Fuels	2,675	8,327	65,618	58,925	60,337
Coal	518	1,354	5,782	4,877	5,311
Petroleum	1,685	6,000	46,274	40,063	39,379
Chemicals	690	1,865	6,824	7,207	8,346
Machinery and Equipment	1,326	3,486	9,112	10,409	12,066
Manufactured Goods, total	3,517	11,494	29,556	31,220	—
Imports, total	**12,987**	**38,314**	**131,931**	**126,393**	**136,503**

Source: Japan Tariff Association. *The Summary Report: Trade of Japan.*

Directions: After studying the table, list each of the 12 products, and designate Japan's usage of each.

Scarcity: Natural Resources

Japan's Food Demand and Supply in 1982 (1,000 metric tons)

Product	Domestic Production[1]	Foreign Trade		Domestic Consumption[2]	Self-Sufficiency Ratio[1,2]
		Imports	Exports		
Cereals	11.433	24.927	358	36.647	31%
Rice	10.270	61	348	10.988	93
Wheat	742	5.432	10	6.035	12
Maize (Corn)	2	14.206	—	13.791	0
Pulses[3]	431	4.659	13	5.036	9
Vegetables	16.646	411	3	17.054	98
Fruit	6.218	1.680	101	7.860	79
Meat	3.135	783	3	3.934	80
Hens' Eggs	2.069	41	0	2.110	98
Cows' Milk[4]	6.844	1.085	6	8.074	85
Fish & Shellfish	10.784	1.527	1.263	11.325	95
Fats & Oils	1.940	464	189	2.215	88
Soy Sauce	1.272	0	8	1.262	101

[1] Includes both domestic and imported inputs, such as feed and raw materials.
[2] Domestic consumption = domestic production + imports − exports +/− changes in stocks.
[3] Edible seeds of plants having pods.
[4] Includes dairy products.
Source: Ministry of Agriculture, Forestry and Fisheries. Japan.

Directions: Select several of the food items from the table above. Compare food demand (consumption) and food supply (production) for different foods. What, if any, are the economic implications of the consumption patterns?

Scarcity: Natural Resources

Imports of Foodstuffs by Country (U.S. $ millions)

Importing Country	Percent of Total Imports	Meat & Meat Preparations	Dairy Products & Birds' Eggs	Fish & Fish Products	Cereals & Cereal Preparations	Vegetables & Fruit	Fancy Foods	Beverages	Tobacco
U.S.A.	7.6%	2,242	439	3,764	340	3,358	4,142	2,948	761
West Germany	11.0	2,056	1,650	628	1,219	4,771	2,335	933	716
Japan	13.1	1,772	243	3,884	4,191	1,613	973	312	533
United Kingdom	12.0	1,992	954	767	903	2,607	1,213	936	523
France	10.5	1,998	435	1,045	787	2,384	1,446	500	507
Italy	13.1	2,278	1,525	607	1,274	689	826	238	468
Netherlands	13.1	358	1,000	195	1,037	1,543	1,067	347	515
Canada	6.6	305	91	353	249	1,527	539	274	51
Australia	5.1	13	56	213	38	163	210	87	77
OECD Total*	9.8	14,435	7,809	13,306	13,662	22,158	15,702	7,839	5,216

Source: DECD, *Statistics of Foreign Trade.*

*Organization for Economic Cooperation and Development

Directions: In an assigned group discuss general world imports of foodstuffs. Compare Japan's imports of food to other countries'. Does Japan import more or less of each category of foodstuffs than the U.S. does? Than other countries? What other observations can you make about Japan's food imports in relation to other nations'?

Scarcity: Natural Resources

Questions for Discussion

1. Are the nations of the world becoming more independent? How?

2. How has geography influenced the history and economic development of Asia?

3. What is the relationship between the United States business cycle and world economic activities?

4. How does scarcity affect decision making?

Resources

7

Selected Resources about Japan

The multitude of resources about Japan makes it impossible to be all-inclusive; this list is selective. It includes items that teachers have already found useful; items recommended by the Great Lakes-Japan in the Schools Project team; by travelers to and from Japan; by reliable resources and selection guides; and also many of the items used as background for the preparation of this book.

Of special interest in the print sections is the reference to Yasuko Makino's book, *Japan Through Children's Literature: An Annotated Bibliography*, second edition, Greenwood Press, 1985. The recommendations in this bibliography are widely available in many school and public libraries. Readers will note that references to Makino's book are marked with an asterisk.

Resource Guides for Teaching about Japan

An Introduction to International Trade: Focus on Japan and the U.S. The Japan Project, 1985.

> Focuses on the importance of international trade in our lives, using U.S.-Japan trade as a model. Strategies include data collection, graph creation, role-playing, research, and critical reading. Available from:
>> The Japan Project, SPICE
>> Lou Henry Hoover Building, #200
>> Stanford University
>> Stanford, California 94305-6012

Contemporary Japan: A Teaching Workbook. 1987. (Gr. 7-12)

> A comprehensive supplement to textbooks, with readings, activities, discussion questions, film suggestions, and resource suggestions. Available from:
>> East Asian Curriculum Project
>> Columbia University
>> 420 West 118th Street
>> New York, NY 10027

Intercultural Contact: The Japanese in Rutherford County, Tennessee. Tom Bibler and Lucien Ellington, 1986. (Gr. 7-12)

> This study guide of 12 lessons is designed to accompany a 30-minute videotape about a Japanese owned manufacturing plant in Tennessee. For use in economics, geography, and world studies. Available from:
>> Vicki McNeal
>> University of Tennessee Research Corporation
>> 415 Communication Building
>> University of Tennessee
>> Knoxville, Tennessee 37996-0344
>> (615) 974-1882

Japan. Rita Geiger, 1983. (Gr. K-12)

Overviews of and activities in geography, history, culture, education, government, economics, and industry, plus a resource bibliography. Available from:

Oklahoma State Department of Education
Curriculum Division
2500 North Lincoln Boulevard
Oklahoma City, OK 73105
(405) 521-3361

Japan in American Economics: Teaching Strategies and Resources. Betty Cowley and Jerry D. Johnson, 1987. (Gr. 7-12)

Twenty-three lesson plans with activities designed to supplement the Joint Council on Economic Education's *Teaching About the Japanese Economy.* Includes maps, tables, current newspaper and periodical articles, handouts, pre- and post-tests. Available from:

The Center for Economic Education
c/o Dr. Jerry D. Johnson
University of Wisconsin-Eau Claire
Eau Claire, WI 54701

Japan Resource Book. 1985. (Gr. 5-8)

Contains activities for teaching and learning about Japan through various aspects of daily life. Designed for middle school and junior high students. Available from:

Department of Curriculum
Anne Arundel County Public Schools
2644 Riva Road
Annapolis, Maryland 21401
(301) 224-5000

Junior/Senior High School Level Curriculum Unit. Developed by the Japan Alumni.
Middle School Curriculum Units. Developed by the Japan Alumni.
Elementary Curriculum Units. Developed by the Japan Alumni.
General Reference Materials on Japan.

These materials have been developed by educators who have received fellowships to study in Japan through the National Council for the Social Studies or the U.S. Japan Education Group. A catalogue about the units is available from:

Charles von Loewenfeldt, Inc.
1333 Gough Street, Suite 6F
San Francisco, California 94109

Modern Japan: An Idea Book for K-12 Teachers. Mary H. Bernson and Elaine Magnusson, eds., 1984.

Forty lessons with activities, developed by teachers who visited Japan. Emphasis on social studies and language arts; range of topics includes geography, haiku, folktales, homes, festivals, law and justice. Available from:

Social Studies Development Center
Indiana University
2805 East 10th Street, Room 120
Bloomington, Indiana 47405

Omiyage. Marilyn Turkovich, Peggy Mueller and Linda Bubolz Ashida, 1986. (Gr. 6-12)
   A book of experiences in Japanese language and culture. It uses language activities
   to teach about the culture, history and values of the Japanese people.

Parallel Passages: Contrasting Views from U.S. and Japan. James Becker and Linda
Wojtan, 1987. (Gr. 7-12) Price: $3.00
   Using selected passages from Japanese and U.S. social studies textbooks, this booklet
   presents contrasting views and interpretations of historical events. Available from:
      Social Studies Development Center
      Indiana University
      2805 East 10th Street, Room 120
      Bloomington, Indiana 47405

Perspectives on Japan: A Guide for Teachers. John J. Cogan and Donald O. Schneider,
1983.
   Provides background information, activity ideas and resources to use with students in
   elementary and secondary levels. Includes geography, economics, cultural traditions,
   role of women, religion, and ethics. Available from:
      The National Council for the Social Studies
      3501 Neward Street, N.W.
      Washington, D.C. 20016

Shogun: A Guide for Classroom Use. Prepared by Teaching Japan in the Schools,
Stanford University, 1980. (Gr. 7-12)
   A guide to *Shogun* by James Clavell with a glossary of characters, list of Japanese
   words from the book, geographical notes, lessons on ethnocentrism, maps, handouts,
   background information, historical comparisons, and timeline for Japan and Western
   Europe. Bibliography.

Stepping Stones: Teaching About Japan in Elementary Grades. Compiled by Elgin
Heinz.
   Selected lesson plans from the *Japan Alumni.*

Suggested Activities for Teaching About Japan. Leslie Handley, 1985. ERIC:ed 263-040
(Gr. 1-3) Price: $3.70 plus postage
   Five activities which center on culture and folktales, neighborhoods and communities, comparisons of self and family with those in Japan. Critically annotated bibliography of children's literature appended. Available from:
      ERIC Document Reproduction Services
      3900 Wheeler Avenue
      Arlington, VA 22304-5110
      Toll free: 1-800-227-3742

Tanoshii Gakusho—Learning with Enjoyment. Michele Shoresman and Waunita Kino-
shita, 2nd ed., 1980. (Gr. 1-6)
   A compilation of activities and information for elementary use. Includes maps,
   games, cooking, folktales, art projects. List of teaching resources. Available from:
      The Center for Asian Studies
      1208 West California
      Urbana, Illinois 61801

Von Lowenfeldt, Charles, et al., eds. "Teaching About Japan Through Art and Modern Literature." *Social Education*, 45, 5 (May 1981). (Gr. 7-12) Price: $2.50.

A wealth of background reading, discussion questions, classroom activities in art, literature, language, religion, and contemporary issues. Available from:

The National Council for the Social Studies
3501 Newark Street, N.W.
Washington, D.C. 20016

Teaching About the Japanese Economy: Background Information and Instructional Activities. Armento, Beverly C., et al., eds., 1986. (Gr. 7-12)

Background information about Japanese values and attitudes plus instructional plans and activities on scarcity, labor, trade, productivity, competition, exchange rates and industrial policy. Available from:

The Joint Council on Economic Education
2 Park Avenue
New York, NY 1002

Newsletters and Periodicals

Colloquy
Published by The Bay Area Global Education Program; available free from:
World Affairs Council of Northern California
Joyce Buchholz, Director of School Programs
312 Sutter Street, #200
San Francisco, CA 94108
(415) 982-2541

East Asian Newsletter
University of Wisconsin
1440 Van Hise Hall
Madison, WI 53706
(608) 262-7801

East-West Perspectives
A quarterly journal containing articles on the entire Pacific Basin region as well as Japan. Available from:
The East-West Center
Office of Public Affairs
1777 East-West Road
Honolulu, HI 96848

Focus on Asian Studies
Includes articles and essays on an array of topics, model curricula, book reviews, resources, and a calendar of Asian-related events across the country. Subscription: $8.00 per year (3 issues). Available from:
Focus
P.O. Box 1308-M
Fort Lee, NJ 07024

Japan Pictorial (North American Edition). Subscription: $32.00 per year
Available from:
 Japan Graphic, Inc.
 Palaceside Building 1-1-1
 Hitotsubashi, Chiyoda-Ku
 Tokyo 100, JAPAN

The Japan Foundation Newsletter
Available from:
 The Editor
 The Japan Foundation Newsletter
 Publications Department,
  The Japan Foundation
 Park Building, 3-6 Kioi-cho
 Chiyoda-Ku
 Tokyo 102, JAPAN

Japan Quarterly
An English translation of general interest in arts, culture, economics, politics, history, and literature. Current book reviews and a few colored photographs. Secondary level. Subscription: $30.00/yr. (overseas). Available through U.S. subscription services or from:
 Ashai Shimbun Publishing Company
 5-3-2 Tsukiji
 Chuoku
 Tokyo 104, JAPAN

Japanese Echo
Speaking About Japan
Both of these periodicals contain translations of speeches and articles originally printed for Japanese readers. Sample copies available from:
 Keizai Koho Center
 (Japanese Institute for Social and Economic Affairs)
 6-1, Otemachi 1-chome
 Chiyoda-Ku
 Tokyo 100, JAPAN

The Morikami Newsletter
Contains short articles on Japan's history and culture. (Gr. 6-12) Available from:
 The Morikami Newsletter
 4000 Morikami Park Road
 Delray Beach, FA 33446
 (305) 499-0631

Teaching About Japan Newsletter. Available from:
 Five-College Center for East Asian Studies
 97 Spring Street
 Box 740
 Amherst, MA 01002
 (413) 256-8316

Selected Periodicals and Articles

The number of articles about Japan appearing in periodicals and journals during the last two or three years has been overwhelming and certainly attests to the great importance of Japan, as well as American readers' interest in the country. Narrowing the selection into a usable list for teachers has been a formidable task; these were used as sources of consultation for this guidebook. An attempt was made to list articles that might be available in school or public libraries rather than to provide those from obscure sources and to use current sources so that the information would be as up-to-date as possible.

Abiko, Tashahiko and Paul L. George. "Education for Early Adolescents in Japan, U.S.: Cross Cultural Observations." *NASSP Bulletin*, 70, 494 (December 1986), pp. 74-81.

"Appreciating Another Culture." *Learning 86*, 14, 7 (March 1986), pp. 73-82. (Poster with teaching guide).

Balzer, Robert Lawrence. "Made in Japan." *Travel-Holiday*, 166, 3 (September 1986), pp. 60-61 +.

Cogan, John and Walter Enloe. "The Japanese History Textbook Controversy Revisited." *Social Education*, 51, 7 (October 1987), pp. 450 +.

Copeland, Jeff B., et al. "How to Win Over a Japanese Boss." *Newsweek*, 109, 2 (February 2, 1987), pp. 46-48.

Crowe, Chris. "Overcoming Ethnocentrism: Teaching Japan in English Class." *English Journal*, 76, 7 (November 1987), pp. 38-40.

Deasy, Richard J. "Education in Japan: Surprising Lessons." *Educational Leadership*, 44, 1 (September 1986), pp. 38-43.

Debbs, Stephen Mark. "Japan Trail '83: American Art Odyssey to the Orient." *Art Education*, 36, 6 (November 1983), pp. 4-11.

Enloe, Walter and Philip Lewin. "The Cooperative Spirit in Japanese Primary Education." *The Educational Forum*, 51, 3 (Spring 1987), pp. 233-247.

Ginocchio, Frederick L. "Nurturing Integrative Thinking: Poetry in Social Studies." *The Social Studies*, 73, 3 (May/June 1987), pp. 123-126.

Gabauer, George. "In the Shortness of a Breath . . . Haiku and Nature Interpretation." *Journal of Outdoor Education*, 19 (1984-85), pp. 25-27. (Published by Northern Illinois University, DeKalb, Illinois).

Granes, William. "Tokyo: A Profile of Success." *National Geographic*, 170, 5 (November 1986), pp. 606-45.

Gregg, N. Taylor. "Hagi: Where Japan's Revolution Began." *National Geographic*, 165, 6 (June 1984), pp. 751-772.

Hantula, James. "Learning About Japan in the Secondary School." *Journal of Social Studies Research*, 10, 2 (Fall 1986), pp. 13-26.

Inamura, Anne E. "Back to Basics: The Family and the School in Japan." *Wisconsin International Trade Magazine*, (November/ December 1987), pp. 10-13.

Lord, Lewis J., et al. "The Brain Battle." *U.S. News and World Report*, 102, 2 (January 19, 1987), pp. 58-64.

"Making Seals and Insignias." *Learning 86*, 14, 7 (March 1986), pp. 35-36. (Includes reproducible designs for family crests).

McCarry, Charles. "The Japan Alps." *National Geographic*, 166, 2 (August 1984), pp. 238-259.

Merrick, Bill. "Japan Trade Mission is Successful for Wisconsin Businesses." *Wisconsin International Trade Magazine*, (July/August 1987), p. 27.

Nishimura Hidetoshi. "Universities Under Pressure to Change." *Japan Quarterly*, 34, 2 (April-June 1987), pp. 204-210.

O'Connor, Patrick J. "Recommended: Ryunosuke Akutagawa." *English Journal*, 75, 7 (November 1986), pp. 7-80.

Okim, Victor E. "Legalistic Approach to U.S.-Japan Trade Frictions and Its Consequences." *Wisconsin International Trade Magazine*, (July/August 1986), pp. 2-3.

Paleologos, Nicholas. "Pacific Overtures." *Phi Delta Kappan*, 68, 5 (January 1987), pp. 368.

Philip Richard, "Out of Darkness: Butoh (Part 1), Kazuo Ohns." *Dance Magazine*, 60, 4 (April 1986), pp. 61-63.

Powell, Bill. "Is Japan as Rich as You Think?" *The Mailbox* (Primary Edition), 10, 2 (March/April 1988).

Schwartz, Debra M. "Teaching Social Studies through Art: Japan: A Case Study." *Social Education*, 45, 5 (May 1981), pp. 333-350.

Simons, Carol. "They Get By with a Lot of Help from Their Kyoiku Mamas." *Smithsonian*, 17, 3 (March 1987), pp. 44-53.

Stein, Bonnie Sue. "Out of Darkness: Butoh (Part 2), Sankai Juko." *Dance Magazine*, 60, 4 ("April 1986), pp. 64-68.

Stinchecum, Amanda Mayer. "Osaka: A Lesson in Japanese Character." *Travel-Holiday*, 167, 4 (April 1987), pp. 64-68.

Stinchecum, Amanda Mayer. "Ryokan: The Japanese Inn." *Travel-Holiday*, 168, 5 (November 1987), pp. 60-65.

Tsutsui, Michio. "Five Beloved Folktales and Their Trees." *Japan Quarterly*, 34, 2 (April-June 1987), pp. 204-210.

Bibliographies

Free Resources for Teaching About Japan. Linda S. Wojtan, revised ed., 1985.
> Contains information and addresses for obtaining free resource materials such as booklets, pamphlets, films. K-12 teaching ideas related to economics, history, environment are also included. Available from:
>> East Asian Studies Center at Indiana University
>> 205 Memorial Hall West
>> Bloomington, Indiana 47405

Guide to Recommended Curriculum and Audio-Visual Materials for Teaching About Japan. Linda S. Wojtan, 1986.
> Includes: Curriculum materials, audio-visual resources, reference materials for elementary and secondary levels, casts, rental fees, addresses and telephone numbers in addition to annotations for each item. Available from:
>> The Midwest Program for Teaching about Japan
>> Indiana University
>> 2805 East Tenth Street
>> Bloomington, Indiana 47405

Japan Database. Fred Czarra. The Council of Chief State School Offices, 1986. Price: $20.00

A resource guide containing sources on K-12 curriculum materials, organizations, and institutes offering Japanese resources and programs. Available from:

The Japan Database Project
Council of Chief State School Offices
379 Hall of the States
400 North Capitol St., N.W.
Washington, D.C. 20001
(202) 393-8161

Japan for Westerners. Chris Popence. Yes! Inc., 1986.

A current annotated bibliography of books about Japan arranged topically by arts, music, literature, history, language, etc. Author index and publishers' addresses included. Available from:

Yes! Inc.
1035 31st Street, N.W.
Washington, D.C. 20007-4482

Japan Through Children's Literature. Yasuko Makino, 2nd ed. Greenwood Press, 1985.

Critical annotated reviews of books from primary through high school levels. Sections focus on art, drama, music, fiction, poetry, folklore, social studies, and background reading. Indexed by title and author. Glossary appended. Available from:

Greenwood Press
88 Post Road W
P.O. Box 5007
Westport, Connecticut 06881
    or
The Asia Society
Educational Resource Program
133 East 58th Street
New York, NY 10022

List of Publications: Governmental and Similars. (Japanese) Government Publications Service Center, 1987.

A list of titles, sources, and prices of Japanese government publications that are available in English. Areas of interest include law, foreign affairs, economics, labor, transportation, education, and health. Some items are free. Available from:

Government Publications Service Center
Z-1, 1-chome
Kasumigaseki, Chiyoda-ku
Tokyo, Japan

Teaching About Asia. Linda S. Wojtan, (undated).

Includes ERIC resources about East Asia, dated as recently as 1986, ERIC document numbers, prices for microfiche and paper copies, plus annotation for each item. Addresses of Asian professional organizations and university outreach programs on Asian studies are also available. Available from:

Social Studies Development Center
2805 East 10th Street, Suite 120
Indiana University
Bloomington, Indiana 47405
(812) 335-3838

Reference Resources

Bisignani, J.D. *Japan Handbook*. Moon Publications, 1983.
  A background survey and travel guide which includes extensive and detailed information on Japan, the language, history, and culture. Travel information on large cities, individual districts, and special points of interest for visitors. Schedules of festivals and other events are given special attention. Maps and black and white photographs. Secondary level.

Discover Japan: Words, Customs and Concepts. Vols. 1 and 2. Kodansha International, 1982.
  A broad and arbitrary collection of reflections about customs, concepts, and Japanese words, written by non-Japanese who have lived and shared in the country's culture. The topics cover a wide range, from "nigirimeshi" (rice ball) to "koto" (a stringed instrument); festivals, foods, footware, and family customs are also surveyed. Many photographs. General reading level.

Kodansha Encyclopedia of Japan. Kodansha Ltd., 1983. Supplement, 1986.
  Nine volumes with index. "The first effort in the world to compile an encyclopedia about Japan in English . . . ." Covers history, art, literature, social sciences, scientific technology, biographical information, and many topics relevant to contemporary Japan. General reading level which meets the needs of upper elementary through secondary students.

Pictorial Encyclopedia of Modern Japan, edited by Akira Kubota, and others. Gakken (Tokyo), 1986.
  Through text, facts, figures, graphs, charts, and tables, Japan's technology, industry, business, everyday life, and culture are surveyed. Extensive graphics show Japan's relationship to the rest of the world in trade, population, economics, social services, agriculture, finance. Detailed photographs. General reading level.

Fiction

Ariyoshi, Sawako. *The Doctor's Wife*, trans. Wakako Hironaka and Ann Siller Kosatant. Kodansha International, 1979.*

The story of a Japanese doctor and his family in the late 1700s and early 1800s. Professional success leads to conflicts between his mother and his wife. Makino recommends this for studies of family and women in Japan. (Gr. 9+)

Buck, Pearl. *The Big Wave*. John Day, 1947.

A classic story about life and death, set in Japan during the occurrence of an enormous tidal wave that sweeps away homes and people. (Gr. 4-6)

Clavell, James. *Shogun: A Novel of Japan*. Atheneum, 1975.

An epic tale, well-known through the televised version. The story is about Englishman Will Adanis and the feudal lords of seventeenth century Japan, who are locked in a power struggle. (Gr. 10-adult)

Clement, Claude. *The Painter and the Wild Swans*. Dial, 1986.

A Japanese painter leaves his work to pursue wild swans that have captivated his attention, but he faces death when he finds them on an island in an icy lake. Delicate paintings and Japanese calligraphy add to the beauty of the transformation story. (Gr. K+)

Coerr, Eleanor. *Sadako and the Thousand Paper Cranes*. Putnam, 1977.

Eleven-year-old Sadako struggles with leukemia after the Hiroshima bombing. If she makes 1,000 paper cranes, according to a legend, she will become well. A memorable and warm story. (Gr. 3-5)

Floethe, Louise Lee. *A Thousand and One Buddhas*. Farrar, 1967.*

Emperor Goshirakawa ordered a beautiful temple with 1,001 Buddha statues to be built in Kyoto, the ancient capital, with the hope of inspiring his people to live in spiritual peace. Those statues may still be seen today. Both author and illustrator paid close attention to historical evidence in settings, customs, and clothing of twelfth century Japan. (Gr. K-4)

Fortune, J.J. *Duel for the Samurai Sword*. Laurel-Leaf Library/Dell, 1984.*

An exciting, if not very realistic, story in a contemporary setting in Tokyo. Stephen, Uncle Richard, and Aka have dangerous encounters while attempting to protect a Masamune sword from a gangster. Japanese words and sentences included; illustrated. (Gr. 5-9)

Friedman, Ina R. *How My Parents Learned to Eat*. Houghton Mifflin, 1984.

A Japanese woman and her American sailor boyfriend attempt to learn about the other's way of eating. A gentle story told from their daughter's point of view. (Gr. 1-3)

---

* Annotations followed by an asterisk have been paraphrased from, *Japan Through Children's Literature: An Annotated Bibliography*, 2nd ed., Yasuko Makino ed., Greenwood Press, 1985.

Garrison, Christian. *The Dream Eater*. Bradbury Press, 1978.*

A *baku,* a mythical animal that lives on bad dreams, is saved from dying of hunger by a little Japanese boy while the villagers sleep. The illustrations by Diane Goode are beautiful, but it should be noted that there are a mixture of Japanese and Chinese elements. (Gr. 1-3)

Guest, Lynn. *The Sword of Hachiman: A Novel of Early Japan*. McGraw-Hill, 1981.*

The story of Minamoto no Yoshitsune, younger brother of Japan's first shogun, and a popular hero in Japanese history. This exciting story is about the power struggle between the warriors and the nobility. (Gr. 9+)

Hamada, Hirosuke. *The Dragon's Tears: Picture Play for Kindergarten, School, and Home*. Tuttle, 1964.*

This book is presented in a picture-play format, known as *kamishibai,* meaning *paper play,* and is highly recommended for classroom use. Excellent illustrations on 16 panels. (Gr. K-2)

Haugaard, Erik Christian. *The Samurai's Tale*. Houghton Mifflin, 1984.

After his family is killed, Murakami is renamed and led off by his captors to serve a samurai. From his life as a favored son to that of a captive, and later a trusted aide of a noble, he faces new challenges in turbulent Japan of the sixteenth century. (Gr. 5-9)

Laurin, Anne. *Perfect Crane*. Harper and Row, 1981.

A lonely Japanese magician brings his origami crane to life, but when autumn arrives he must set the bird free. The gesture opens up a new beginning for the magician and leads to friendship and love. (Gr. 2-6)

Luenn, Nancy. *The Dragon Kite*. Harcourt, Brace, Jovanovich, 1982. (Ill. by Michael Hague)

Ishikawa, a Robin Hood-type character, learns to build a kite, then attempts to steal the golden dolphins atop the shogun's castle so he can distribute the wealth to the peasants. Rich illustrations of Japanese culture. (Gr. 3-5)

Namioka, Lensey. *The Samurai and the Long-Nosed Devils*. McKay, 1976.*

An historically accurate and exciting book, this is one of a series of mystery and adventure stories about two *ronin* or masterless samurai. Set in the sixteenth century, it provides an introduction to samurai life and the honor code of the warrior class. Other books in this series by the same author are also highly recommended: *Valley of the Broken Cherry Trees* (1980), *Village of the Vampire Cat* (1981), and *White Serpent Castle* (1976). (Gr. 5+)

Nikly, Michelle. *The Emperor's Plum Tree*, trans. Elizabeth Shub. Greenwillow, 1982.

Delicate Oriental-style watercolors illustrate the story of a plum tree whose owners are lamenting its loss to the emperor's garden. (Gr. K-3)

Paterson, Katherine. *The Master Puppeteer*. Crowell, 1975.

A mystery set in eighteenth century feudal Japan depicts the world of the puppet theater as well as the lawlessness of the times. (Gr. 6-9)

Say, Allen. *The Bicycle Man*. Parnassus Press, 1982.
   The author-illustrator remembers a day from his childhood in Japan when an American soldier came to his school and did tricks on a bicycle. *Horn Book* calls this a story that "celebrates human friendship." (Gr. K-3)

Say, Allen. *The Feast of Lanterns*. Harper and Row, 1976.*
   A story of two young brothers who live in a fishing village on a small Japanese island. Longing to see the mainland, they take their uncle's boat on the Feast of Lanterns, but find the reality there is nothing like their dreams. Highly recommended; authentic and detailed illustrations. (Gr. K-4)

Say, Allen. *The Ink-Keeper's Apprentice*. Harper and Row, 1979.
   Thirteen-year-old Kiyoi, living on his own in postwar Tokyo, becomes apprenticed to a well-known cartoonist and experiences a clash between some of the traditions and the challenges of changing times and the future. (Gr. 7+)

Tsuboi, Sakae. *Twenty-four Eyes*, trans. Akira Miura. Tuttle, 1983.*
   A touching story of an elementary teacher and her 12 pupils during the years 1926 to 1946. By following the children's lives through these years, the author points out the inhumanity of war. According to Makino, the translation by Akira Miura is well done. Made into a popular movie in Japan. (Gr. 3-12)

Uchida, Yoshiko. *Sumi and the Goat and the Tokyo Express*. Scribner, 1969.
   The new high-speed train wasn't supposed to stop at Sugi Village, but the schedule didn't take into account Miki, the goat. (Gr. K-4)

Watkins, Yoko Kawashima. *So Far From the Bamboo Grove*. Lothrop, Lee and Shepard, 1986.
   Eleven-year-old Yoko, her mother, and older sister escape from Korea at the end of World War II to return to their home in Japan. This is the story of their frightening adventures as refugees as well as the separate flight of their brother Hideyo, who made his own way back to an eventual reunion with his sisters. A good story to capture the idea of Japanese family relationships. (Gr. 6+)

Winthrop, Elizabeth. *Journey to the Bright Kingdom*. Holiday House, 1979.
   Based on the legend of the rolling rice cakes, a blind woman regains her vision and sees her daughter for the first time. (Gr. 2-4)

Zimelman, Nathan. *Look, Hiroshi!* Aurora Publishers (Nashville), 1973, c1972.
   Hiroshi's five-year-old sister helps him discover the world around him through her imaginative "seeing." Woodcut illustrations present ideas for creative writing. (Gr. K-3)

Nonfiction

Ashby, Gwynneth. *Take a Trip to Japan.* Franklin Watts, 1980.
   Colored photos show the customs of Japanese children, families, homes, communities, religious and cultural traditions, occupations, recreations, transportation, and geography. (Gr. 1-3)

Beasley, W.G. *The Modern History of Japan.* 3rd ed. Holt, 1981.*
   A detailed history of nineteenth and twentieth century that is strong on foreign relations. Recommended for advanced students. (Gr. 10+)

Blumberg, Rhoda. *Commodore Perry in the Land of the Shogun.* Lothrop, Lee and Shepard, 1985.
   Details Commodore Matthew Perry's role in opening Japan's closed society to world trade in the 1850s in one of the most significant diplomatic achievements in history. Excellent bibliography, notes, and appendices. Newberry Medal Honor Book, 1986. (Gr. 5+)

Cohen, Stephen D. *Uneasy Partnership: Competition and Conflict in U.S.-Japan Trade Relations.* Ballinger Publishing, 1985.
   A review of the nature and causes of U.S.-Japanese trade problems, contemporary bilateral trade relations, foreign trade performance, economic policies, the perceptions about each country's trade attitudes, and a look at the future. (Secondary)

Davidson, Judith. *Japan, Where East Meets West.* Dillon, 1983.
   Describes what it's like to be Japanese. Includes details for units of study, including symbols, food and recipes, clothing. Consulate addresses included. (Gr. 5-7)

A Day in the Life of Japan. Collins, 1985.
   This book of colored photographs, taken by 100 of the world's leading photojournalists, presents a kaleidoscope of Japan from "geisha to gangsters, cityscapes to countryside." A coffee table book that would be of great interest in the school library. (All levels)

De Mente, Boye. *The Whole Japan Book: An Encyclopedic Reader on Things Japanese.* Phoenix Books, 1983.
   Described as "a treasure trove of fascinating facts and insights," this encyclopedia includes 800 Japanese-related terms and a descriptive paragraph or essay about each. Though not all-inclusive, it is an excellent and handy reference guide; the photographs, pronunciation guides, index, and addresses of sources are additional aids to the reader. (Gr. 10+)

Deutsch, Mitchell F. *Doing Business with the Japanese.* The New American Library, 1983.
   Cross-cultural observations written with the objective to ward off superstitions, prejudice, and misunderstandings. Problems and their solutions regarding conducting business with Japanese firms. Written from the point of view of an American who has

worked within the Japanese business structure. Pragmatic, not theoretical. (Secondary)

Dolan, Edward F., Jr., and Shan Finney. *The New Japan*. Franklin Watts, 1983.
The culture of modern Japan in a readable text with a few black and white photos. Discusses factors which contribute to harmony in the workplace, the family, and the school. Old traditions are contrasted with new ideas; old behavior models are criticized by the young. A look at change in Japan. (Gr. 7-9)

Earhart, H. Byron. *Religions of Japan*. Harper and Row, 1984.
After an introduction to Japan, this book focuses on Shinto, Buddhism, Taoism, Confucianism, Christianity, folk religions, and the New Religions. Also included are religious practices, festivals, and the role of religion in the lives of the Japanese. (Secondary)

Elkin, Judith. *A Family in Japan*. Lerner, 1987.
Young readers will find many similarities and differences between Japanese and American family life in this portrait of family life in Japan through the lives of two brothers, Daisuke and Kengo. Excellent colored photos, extensive use of Japanese words (and an appended pronunciation guide), explanations of traditions, festivals, and daily customs give a realistic picture of contemporary Japanese life. (Gr. 2-6)

Greene, Carol. *Japan*. Children's Press, 1983.
Describes the geography, history, scenic treasures, culture, industry, and people of Japan. Maps and excellent colored photos, time-line, a list of important people, and a bibliography. (Gr. 4-6)

Haskins, Jim. *Count Your Way Through Japan*. Carolrhoda Books, 1987.
An illustrated counting book that will enhance a social studies unit on Japan, this book gives an explanation of the Chinese origin of the Japanese number system, then offers interesting facts about Japanese life and culture for each number. (Gr. 2-6)

Jacobsen, Karen. *Japan*. Children's Press, 1982.
The geography, history, and culture of Japan are presented through photographs and simple text. A introduction for primary level. (Gr. 1-3)

Japan Culture Institute, ed. *A Hundred Things Japanese*. The Japan Culture Institute (Tokyo), 1980.
This book, along with its companion, *A Hundred More Things Japanese*, by Hyoe Murakami and Donald Riche (Japan Culture Institute, 1980), offers explanations and illustrations of Japanese festivals, customs, foods, types of entertainment and recreation, and much more. Each two-page text is easy to read and provides details often not found in other research sources. (Gr. 7 +)

Knight, Joan. *Journey to Japan*. Viking Kestrel, 1986.
This clever book with its pop-up format offers the classroom teacher and students a glimpse into the typical Japanese home, the shrine at Nara, an auto assembly plant, and several other scenes. The text provides introductory background information. (Gr. 2-6)

Lifton, Betty Jean. *A Place Called Hiroshima*. Kodansha International, 1985.
The author returns to Hiroshima to record in photos the survivors and rebuilding of the city victimized by the atom bomb. Focuses on the people; a hope for peace. (Gr. 7-12)

Maruki, Toshi. *Hiroshima No Pika*. Lothop, Lee and Shepard, 1980 [1982].
An artistic rendition with simple text of what happened to a family in Hiroshima in 1945 when the atom bomb destroyed the city. Told from the viewpoint of a mother. (Gr. 5+)

The Pacific War Research Society, ed. *Japan's Longest Day*. Kodansha International, 1986.*
The story of the 24-hour period that preceded Emperor Hirohito's radio broadcast on August 15, 1945, in which he announced Japan's surrender to the Allies. (Gr. 9+)

Perry, John Curtis. *Beneath the Eagle's Wings: Americans in Occupied Japan*. Dodd, Mead, 1980.*
The title is descriptive, but Makino adds that this is "a sensitive analysis" of the period between August 1945 and the spring of 1952. The book includes many photographs not available in other books, detailed notes, and a bibliography. (Gr. 10+)

Reischauer, Edwin O. *Japan: The History of the Nation*. 3rd ed. Knopf, 1981.

Richie, Donald. *A Taste of Japan*. Kodansha, 1985. (Distributed through Harper and Row)
Covers Japanese food facts and fables, what people eat, their customs, and etiquette. Although recipes are not included, there are beautiful photographs of Japanese food arrangements. (Secondary)

Roberson, John K. *Japan from Shogun to Sony, 1543-1984*. Atheneum, 1985.
This historical account focuses on Japan's relations with other countries and how their policies brought about changes. Photographs, old prints, plus a bibliography. (Gr. 8+)

Runkle, Scott F. *An Introduction to Japanese History*. International Society for Educational Information Press, 1976.
Briefly covers the history of the classical, feudal, and modern periods. (Gr. 6-12)

Tames, Richard. *Japan in the Twentieth Century*. Batsford Academic and Educational Ltd., 1981.
A readable text about Japan with many maps and black and white photos. Discussion questions at the end of each chapter. (Gr. 6-8)

Thurley, Elizabeth F. *Through the Year in Japan*. Batsford, 1986.
An in-depth look at daily life in Japan, organized by months. Contains proverbs, recipes, songs, poetry, and statistics. Well-illustrated with photos and pictures. (Gr. 7-12)

Tuttle, Charles E. *Incredible Japan.* C.E. Tuttle, 1975.*
   Makino recommends this as an "informative and humorous introduction to everyday life in Japan." Cartoons accompany the short explanations about customs, clothing, houses, legends, and amusements. (Gr. 7+)

Arts, Crafts, Cooking, and Festivals

Araki, Chiyo. *Origami for Christmas.* Introduction by Lillian Oppenheimer, Kodansha International, 1983.*
   Traditional Japanese paper folding and the most Western of holidays, Christmas, are combined in this book. Step-by-step instructions are in the first section; materials and instructions for assembling whole arrangements are found in the second part. (All ages)

Araki, Chiyo. *Origami in the Classroom.* C.E. Tuttle, 1965-68. 2 vols.
   Origami patterns of graduated difficulty for various holidays, events, and seasons. (Gr. 4+)

Downer, Lesley. *Japanese Vegetarian Cooking.* Pantheon, 1987.
   A valuable resource for those who want to try Japanese cooking and to learn about Japanese ways before the advent of fast foods. The recipes are generally easy, and instructions are straightforward. Included are tofu dishes, tempura, pickled vegetables, pickled plums, and holiday dishes. (Secondary)

Epstein, Sam and Beryl Epstein. *A Year of Japanese Festivals.* Garrad, 1974.
   Festivals such as *Hina Matsuri* (Doll Festival), the One-Thousand-Person Procession, the Okunchi Festival, and the Peace Festival are described and pictured. Makino states that some of the information is not accurate, making the use of this book somewhat less desirable. (Gr. 2-6)

Hirayama, Hakuho. *Sumi-E: Just for You.* Kodansha International, 1979.*
   Practical, easy to follow instructions for beginners of "one-brush" *sumi-e.* Techniques are explained in detail and accompanied by clear, large illustrations and photos. (Gr. 6+)

Moore, Janet Gaylord. *The Eastern Gate: An Invitation to the Arts of China and Japan.* Collins, 1979.*
   Japanese and Chinese art are compared and characterized and their influences discussed. Artistic traditions are analyzed in light of their historical, social, religious, and literary backgrounds. Also of use to the reader: appended notes, list of illustrations, recommended readings, chronology, glossary, and index. (Gr. 10+)

Nakano, Dokuotei. *Easy Origami.* Viking, 1986.
   A short history of the ancient craft of origami prefaces clear directions for easy and more difficult projects. (Gr. 2-6)

Rathbun, William Jay. *Yo no Bi: The Beauty of Japanese Folk Art.* Seattle: University of Washington Press, 1983.*

An extensive catalog of a 1983 exhibition at the Seattle Art Museum, focusing on functional arts. Everyday articles are shown in clear photos accompanied by information on origin, use, and significance. Bibliography. (Gr. 7+)

Soleillant, Claude. *Japan: Activities and Projects in Color,* trans. Louisa B. Hellegers. Sterling Publishing, 1980.

Detailed instructions with diagrams and colored pictures for making festival decorations, games, costumes. An appendix offers simple recipes and addresses for Japanese Tourist Ministries. (Gr. 3-9)

Stevenson, John. *Yoshitoshi's Thirty-Six Ghosts.* Weatherhill, 1983.*

Full-page color prints depict scenes from traditional Japanese stories that contain elements of the supernatural. The prints are imaginative and bring the old stories, retold on the opposite page, to life. Introduction to the idea of the Japanese ghost, plus detailed notes on the artist and the drawings. (Gr. 5+)

Streeter, Tal. *The Art of the Japanese Kite.* Weatherhill, 1974.*

Not only about kites, this book also is about Japan. Includes a brief history of oriental kites and directions on making and flying them. Many illustrations. The author's love for kites is contagious and makes the book interesting to readers, kite lovers or not. (Gr. 6+)

Weston, Reiko. *Cooking the Japanese Way.* Lerner, 1983.

Colorful photographs plus recipes for traditional Japanese foods; a glossary of cooking terms, list of utensils, and special ingredients is appended. (Gr. 5+)

Poetry

Baron, Virginia Olsen, ed. *The Seasons of Time; Tanka Poetry of Ancient Japan.* Dial Press, 1968.

These translations of ancient Japanese poetry from the fourth through twelfth centuries show that the language of poetry speaks across time and cultures. An introduction and an index of poets provide helpful background for readers. This volume is recommended for use with children who have already been introduced to the haiku form. (Gr. 5+)

DeForest, Charlotte B. *The Prancing Pony: Nursery Rhymes from Japan.* Adapted into English verse for children by C.G. DeForest. Walker, 1967.*

A charming collection of over 50 nursery rhymes that retain the meaning and flavor of the originals despite translation. Effective illustrations *(kusa-e)* include rice-paper cuttings. (Gr. K-6)

Fugiwara no Sadaie, ed. *The Little Treasury of One Hundred People, One Poem Each,* trans. Tom Galt. Princeton University Press, 1982. (Gr. 10+)*

A translation of the most popular anthology of *waka* or *tanka* poems, *Ogura Hyakunin Isshu.* The book is bilingual; each poem is written in calligraphy with a transliteration, a translation, and a commentary. Includes introduction, index, and a glossary of poets. (Gr. 10+)

Kobayashi, Issa. *A Few Flies and I: Haiku by Issa.* eds. Jean Merrill and Ronni Solbert and trans. R.H. Blyth and Nobuyuki Yuasa. Pantheon, 1969.*

A collection of poems by eighteenth century haiku poet Issa. Illustrations are small and give the feeling of *haiga* drawings that accompany haiku. "Children will feel the warmness of this master's heart by listening to these poems." Potentially useful in social studies units. (Gr. 4+)

Lewis, Richard, ed. *In a Spring Garden.* Dial Books for Young Readers, 1976. (Illustrated by Ezra Jack Keats)

A collection of 23 translations of haiku poetry illustrated in watercolor and collage. Representations of writing from seventeenth century to modern times, arranged in the order of a spring day. (Gr. K-6)

Lewis, Richard. *Of This World: A Poet's Life in Poetry.* Dial Press, 1968.*

A biography in poetry, this life of Issa, the famous haiku poet, includes many of his poems. Well-organized with excellent photography. (Gr. 5+)

Several other Lewis compilations are also recommended by Makino: *The Moment of Wonder, A Collection of Chinese and Japanese Poetry* 1964 (Gr. 5+); *There are Two Lives: Poems by Children of Japan,* 1970 (Gr. 1-6); and *The Way of Silence: The Prose and Poetry of Basho,* 1970 (Gr. 5-9).

Matsuo, Basho. *A Haiku Journey: Basho's "Narrow Road to the Far North,"* trans. Tom Galt. Princeton University Press, 1980.*

Exquisite color photos perfectly match the poetics of Basho's text and poems. Excellent translations of both text and poetry. Highly recommended by Makino. (Gr. 10+)

Rexroth, Kenneth and Ikuko Atsumi, ed. and trans. *The Burning Heart: Women Poets of Japan.* Seabury Press, 1977.*

An anthology collected from all periods of Japanese history, written by 77 women poets. Notes on each poet plus a brief survey of Japanese women poets. (Gr. 10+)

Sato, Hiroaki and Watson Burton, eds. and trans. *From the Country of Eight Islands: An Anthology of Japanese Poetry.* University of Washington Press, 1981.*

A collection containing samples of all forms of Japanese poetry from all periods of the country's history. Thomas Rimer, a specialist in Japanese poetry, has written the introduction. (Gr. 10+)

Stewart, Harold. *A Chime of Windbells: A Year of Japanese Poetry in English Verse.* Tuttle, 1981.*

An anthology of haiku poetry illustrated with colored *haiga* paintings. Also included is an essay on haiku by the translator; a bibliography, an index, and explanatory notes for the more difficult poems add to the usefulness of this collection. (Gr. 7+)

Ten Thousand Leaves: A Translation of the Man'yoshu, Japan's Premier Anthology of Classical Poetry. Princeton Library of Asian Translations. Translated by Ian Hideo Levy. Princeton University Press, 1981-. Vol. 1.

> This collection is a translation of Man'yoshu poems written by people from all walks of life, compiled in the eighth century. Includes an extensive introduction by the translator. (Gr. 9+)

Folktales

Bartoli, Jennifer. *The Story of the Grateful Crane.* Whitman, 1977.

> Retells the story of a crane who repays an elderly childless couple for rescuing him from a trap. (Gr. K-2)

Brenner, Barbara. *Little One Inch.* Coward, McCann, and Geoghegan, 1977.

> Similar to the story of Issunboshi. Little One Inch defeats several demons through his cunning and bravery. Soft Oriental illustrations evoke a feeling of Japanese culture. (Gr. K-3)

Fisher, Sally. *The Tale of the Shining Princess.* Metropolitan Museum of Art (New York), and the Viking Press, 1980.*

> Recommended by Makino as "one of the best books." This tenth-century story parallels many folk tales from other countries: a young woman assigns impossible tasks to her suitors, promising to marry the one who succeeds. The illustrations are reproduced from an eighteenth-century edition of *Taketori Monogatari* held by the Metropolitan Museum of Art. (Gr. 2-9)

Folk Tales of Old Japan. The Japan Times (Tokyo), 1975.

> A collection of 16 folk tales which were told through the centuries and are still popular today. Includes an appendix of background notes about each tale. (Gr. K-6)

Hearn, Lafcadio. *In Ghostly Japan.* Tuttle, 1979.*

> A collection of 12 Japanese ghost stories, skillfully retold by Hearn. Makino suggests that these would be interesting to the Western reader since they are very different from Western ghost tales. (Gr. 9+)

Japanese Fairy Tales by Lafcadio Hearn and Others. Core Collection Books (Great Neck, N.Y.), 1979.*

> A reprint edition of 20 fairy tales retold by American scholars of Japan. These difficult-to-find stories are well-written and authentic. The large print and easy reading level also will encourage use in special classes. (Gr. 4-9)

Lifton, Betty Jean. *The Mud Snail Son.* Atheneum, 1971.*

> Cited by Makino as "an excellent book to explain Japanese culture and values to young children," this is a transformation tale about an older couple who long for a child of their own. A mud snail is born; he works, marries, and eventually becomes a handsome prince. Recommended because of its beautiful illustrations, plus its retention of the tale's original flavor. (Gr. K-3)

Matsutani, Miyoko. *The Crane Maiden*. English version by Alvin Tresselt. Parents' Magazine Press, 1968.*

This title as well as those listed below are highly recommended by Makino for use with American students, despite occasional mistakes in translations or literary interpretations. (One example is the incorrect use of the honorific "san" in speaking of oneself.) This version of *The Crane Maiden* with its illustrations by Chihiro Iwasaki could be compared with Yagawa's *The Crane Wife* and Bartoli's *The Story of the Grateful Crane*. (Gr. K-3)

Other tales by Matsutani include:

The Fox Wedding. Encyclopedia Britannica, 1963. (Gr. 1-4)

Gengoroh and the Thunder God. Parents' Magazine Press, 1970. (Gr. K-3)

How the Withered Trees Blossomed. Lippincott, 1971. (Gr. K-3)

Taro, the Dragon-Boy. Kodansha International, 1967. (Gr. 3-6)

The Witch's Magic Cloth. Parents' Magazine Press, 1969. (Gr. K-2)

McDermott, Gerald. *The Stonecutter*. Viking, 1975.

The poor stonecutter, Tasaku, wishes for wealth and power, but his greed for more eventually leads to his downfall. Illustrations based on traditional Japanese motifs. (Gr. K-3)

Morimoto, Junko. *The Inch Boy*. Viking Kestrel, 1986.

The inch-high boy vanquishes the dreaded red demon through bravery and intellect. Large, bold illustrations include a full-page Buddha. (Gr. K-2)

Mosel, Arlene. *The Funny Little Woman*. Dutton, 1972.

A Caldecott winner. The little woman outsmarts the wicked "Oni" and keeps on laughing after she escapes from their underground cavern. (Gr. K-2)

Newton, Patricia Montgomery. *The Five Sparrows*. Atheneum, 1982.

An old woman is rewarded for her kindness to a wounded sparrow, but her neighbor, motivated by greed, is repaid in kind. (Gr. 1-4)

Say, Allen. *Once Upon the Cherry Blossoms Tree: An Old Japanese Tale*. Harper and Row, 1974.*

Recommended as a well-told and funny tale, this is an original story about the formation of a lake. A miserly and mean landlord collected too much rent from the peasants. One day, after he swallowed a cherry pit, a tree grew from his head. When he pulled it out, a fishing hole formed. Finally, the landlord disappeared, and all that was left was a lovely lake. (Gr. K-4)

Seki, Keigo. *Folktales of Japan*, trans. Robert J. Adams. University of Chicago Press, 1963.*

The publication date may make this collection harder to obtain, but this collection of 63 common Japanese tales would be excellent to use with secondary students. The six sections are divided by theme: animal tales, ogres, supernatural husbands and wives, kindness rewarded and punished, good fortune, cleverness, and stupidity. The many extra study notes will enhance its usefulness and the reader's enjoyment. (Gr. 10+)

Shute, Linda. *Momotaro, the Peach Boy.* Lothrop, Lee and Shepard, 1986.
Found floating on the river inside a peach, tiny Momotaro grows up to fight the demons who have been terrorizing the village. (Gr. K-2)

Stamm, Claus. *Three Strong Women: A Tall Tale From Japan.* Viking, 1974.
A delightfully funny tale about a wrestler who meets three women who are stronger than he. A turn-around tale that could be used to compare with others in its genre as well for a glimmer into Japanese customs.

Uchida, Yoshiko. *The Magic Listening Cap; More Folk Tales from Japan.* Harcourt, Brace and World, c1955, 1963.
Fourteen Japanese folk tales, several of which have counterparts in other folklore. Many suitable for reading aloud. (Gr. 3-6)

Ury, Marian. *Tales of Times Now Past: Sixty-two Stories from a Medieval Japanese Collection.* University of California Press (Berkeley), 1979.*
Selected from a collection of 1,000 tales from medieval Japan—*Konjaku Monogatarishu;* many of the stories have a "strong religious tone." This is an excellent resource tool with introductory and explanatory notes as well as a bibliography of the texts and translations of the original source. (Gr. 10+)

Wakana, Kei, illus. *The Magic Hat.* Scroll Press, 1970.*
Though this story may be difficult to obtain, those who are able to find it will enjoy the humorous tale in which a man can understand animals by putting on a magic cap. Classroom teachers may wish to use the book with Uchida's *The Magic Listening Cap.* This book offers something special: it is bilingual, printed in Japanese style, and opens from the back. (Gr. K-3)

Yagawa, Sumiko. *The Crane Wife,* trans. Katherine Paterson. Morrow, 1981.*
After Yohei tends a wounded crane, a beautiful young woman begs to become his wife and weaves an exquisite silken fabric for him on her loom. He breaks his promise to not watch her weave, and this causes his enchanted wife to leave. The story is familiar and a favorite of elementary students. Makino highly recommends this version because of Paterson's ability to retain the original Japanese onomatopoeia, which adds a rhythmic effect when read aloud. The illustrations are also outstanding. A perfect book to read aloud to a small group. (Gr. K-4)

Yanagita, Kunio. *The Legends of Tono,* trans. Ronald A. Morse. The Japan Foundation (Tokyo), 1975.*
A collection of over 100 legends from a mountain village storyteller, this volume could be compared to the Grimm brothers' collection. The tales of *tengu,* demons, goblins, and other imaginary creatures are short, and some are similar to Western legends. To help non-Japanese readers, maps and illustrations are included. Originally published in 1910. (Gr. 5+)

Yashima, Taro. *Seashore Story.* Viking, 1967.
In this legend Urashima, the fisherman, is carried off to the palace under the ocean by a turtle. As in the legend of Rip Van Winkle, the world has changed by the time Urashima finally returns to his home. Used with Miyoko Matsutani's version of the same tale, this book will invite discussion and creative writing extensions. (Gr. K-2)

Folktale Dramatizations:

Hall, Margaret, C. "The Mysterious Mirror." *Plays*, 38, 7 (April 1979), pp. 61-64.
  Seeing their reflections brings about surprising results for Kiko and Lili.

Wartski, Maureen Crane, adapter. "Taro the Fisherman." *Plays*, 39, 8 (May 1980), pp. 54-60.
  An orphan makes an incredible journey in this charming fantasy.

Winther, Barbara. "Japanese Trio." *Plays*, 36, 3 (December 1976), pp. 42-49.
  Three witty folktales in the informal style of *kyogen* drama, the short plays presented between the noh drama plays.

Japanese-Americans

Battles, Edith. *What Does the Rooster Say, Yoshio?* Whitman, 1978.
  A Japanese boy and an American girl compare sounds of animals in their own languages and discover that one animal says the same thing to both of them. Animal sounds written in Japanese and English. (Gr. K-2)

Davis, Daniel S., *Behind Barbed Wire: The Imprisonment of Japanese-Americans During World War II.* Dutton, 1982.
  Provides background of Japanese immigration to America, the problems that occurred early in the twentieth century, the prejudicial attitudes, the FBI raids, and fear that led to the internment of Japanese-Americans during the 1940s. The photos and text show how people passed the time during their imprisonment and their eventual reassimilation into society after the war. (Gr. 7+)

Garrigue, Sheila. *The Eternal Spring of Mr. Ito.* Bradbury, 1985.
  The fate of a 200-year-old bonsai tree is decided by a young girl and an old Japanese-Canadian gardener who resists being imprisoned in an internment camp after the bombing of Pearl Harbor. *Voice of Youth Advocates* reviews this as a "beautifully written book with some excellent insights into fear, prejudice, friendship, death, and life." (Gr. 7-9)

Masaoka, Mike M. *They Call Me Moses Masaoka.* Morrow, 1987.
  As the American-born son of Japanese parents, Masaoka was one of the victims of the detention camps in the wake of the Pearl Harbor bombing. Since then he has led many struggles for equal rights. This autobiography tells the story of his efforts to eradicate racism from American immigration laws and his leadership in the Japanese-American Citizens' League. (Secondary)

Miklowitz, Gloria D. *The War Between the Classes.* Delacorte, 1985.
  Amy Sumoto is angered by the racial prejudice engendered by "The Color Game" played in her social studies class. Special understanding and growth occurs in the girl and her traditional, Japanese parents. According to the Interracial Books for Chil-

dren Bulletin, "This interesting novel could provoke dynamic discussions about racism and classism, but a caution must be given about the poor portrayal of the Japanese-American protagonist."

Nelson, Douglas W. *Heart Mountain: The History of American Concentration Camps*. State Historical Society of Wisconsin, 1986.
An analysis of the Japanese-American experience at a concentration camp in Heart Mountain, Wyoming, which was a focal point of draft resistance.

Stein, R. Conrad. *Nisei Regiment*. Childrens Press, 1985.
A history of the 442nd "Nisei" Regiment comprised almost entirely of Japanese-Americans which received more medals for bravery than any other American unit of its size during World War II. (Gr. 6-10)

Uchida, Yoshiko. *The Happiest Ending*. Atheneum, 1985.
Twelve-year-old Rinko tries to intercede when she learns that the daughter of her friend, Auntie Hatu, is coming from Japan to marry a stranger twice her age. But her plan is foiled, and she comes to realize the values of her Japanese ancestry and the strengths of her family and friends. (Gr. 4-8)

Uchida, Yoshiko. *A Jar of Dreams*. Atheneum, 1981.
A young girl grows up in a closely-knit Japanese-American family in California during the 1930s, a time of great prejudice against Japanese. (Gr. 5+)

Uchida, Yoshiko. *Journey Home*. Atheneum, 1978.
After their release from an American concentration camp where they spent the war years, a Japanese-American girl and her family try to reconstruct their lives amidst strong anti-Japanese feeling which bred fear, distrust, and violence. Sequel to *Journey to Topaz*. (Gr. 5+)

Uchida, Yoshiko. *Journey to Topaz*. Scribners, 1971.
Young Japanese-American children living in California find their lives traumatically disrupted when their parents are assumed to be "enemy aliens" after the Pearl Harbor attack. (Gr. 5+)

Weglyn, Michi. *Years of Infamy: The Untold Story of America's Concentration Camps*. William Morrow, 1976.
A firsthand account dealing with the internment of over 110,000 Japanese-Americans who spent the war years behind barbed wire. Original documents cited. (Secondary)

Selected Audio-Visual Resources—Elementary

Only a few, recently-produced audio-visual resources have been selected for this list. These have been recommended by various sources as especially useful. Librarians and teachers will want to consult standard media catalogs and references for additional titles.

#7 Takashima Street. St. Louis, MO: Asia Resources Center.

This unit centers around a Japanese-American family tracing their roots to Suwa, Japan. The children pretend they are members of the Tanaka family, preparing for their first trip to Japan. The unit includes many artifacts, a slide show, numerous classroom activities, and a study of the Bon Festival. (Annotation from Shoresman, *Learning with Enjoyment*) (Gr. 6)

The Haiku Moment: Seeing the World in a Grain of Sand. Stanford, CA: The Japanese Project: SPICE.

Writing activities, accompanied by 12 slides and a cassette tape of haiku and Japanese music, to introduce students to the world of Japanese aesthetics and poetry. (Gr. K-6)

The Rabbit in the Moon: Folktales from China and Japan. Stanford, CA: The Japan Project: SPICE.

A cross-cultural investigation of eight Chinese and Japanese folktales designed to spur student interest in China and Japan. Optional slides are available for two Japanese folktales. Students create their own folktales as a final activity.

Introduction to Japanese: Hirangana. Stanford, CA: The Japan Project: SPICE.

An introduction to the Japanese writing syllabary and to the sounds of the Japanese language. Also includes a pronunciation tape. (Gr. K-6)

Video Letters from Japan. New York, NY: The Asia Society.

This excellent series of 25-minute video programs is designed to give U.S. students a personal, in-depth look at Japan. Japanese students narrate the videos, describing their country to their American counterparts. Accompanying the video letter are a poster and an exceptionally useful teacher's guide, which provides background information, recommended readings, and additional classroom activities. Two videos are packaged in each kit. The titles are: 1) "My Day" and "Tokyo Sunday," 2) "Summer Vacation and "Tohoku Diary," (3) "Making Things" and "My Family," 4) "My Town" and "Japanese History," 5) "Japanese Schools" and "Nature," 6) "Japanese Culture" and "Games and Hobbies." (Gr. 5-7)

If funds are limited, the following titles are recommended as first purchases by the Great Lakes-Japan in the Schools Project:

My Town/Japanese History. Great Lakes-Japan in the Schools Program.

My Family/Making Things. Great Lakes-Japan in the Schools Program.

Tahoku Diary/Summer Vacation. Great Lakes-Japan in the Schools Program.

Selected Audio-Visual Resources-Secondary

Intercultural Contact: The Japanese in Rutherford County, Tennessee. Lucien Ellington, et al. Knoxville, TN: Center for Economic Education.

This 30-minute videotape documentary explores the social and economic ramifications of Japanese investment in Tennessee as well as the Japanese-American interaction in the community. A 12-lesson teacher guide accompanies the tape; useful for economics, geography, world history, multicultural education. (Annotation from Wojtan, *Guide to Recommended Curriculum*, 1986) (Gr. 7-12)

Japan Meets the West: Case Studies of Perceptions. Stanford, CA: The Japan Project: SPICE.

Cultural perceptions are examined through Japan's early contact with the West. Includes 30 slides, primary source readings, and classroom activities. (Gr. 7-12)

The Japan They Don't Talk About. Chicago, IL: Films Incorporated, (NBC White Paper), NBC Television Network. Reported by Lloyd Dobyns; directed by Peter Poor. Videocassette: 60 minutes; VHS 1986.

Argues that the economic miracle of modern Japan, with its giant corporations producing high quality products, is made possible by the lower level of small manufacturing plants operating with cheap labor. (Gr. 9-12)

Japanese Society Through Film. New York, NY: The Japan Society, 1950-1983.

Three videocassettes, color and black and white, 110-135 minutes. Teacher's guide. Reviewed in *School Library Journal* October 1987. (Gr. 7+) Contents: Early Summer. A story of individualism and obligations; centers on the marriage of a daughter (1950). "Mikio Naruse's Mother." Focuses on a mother's sacrifice good of the family (1952). "Family Game." A comic portrayal of a family caught up in the battle of wits with the educational system (1983).

Lifetime Employment. New York, NY: Film Australia. Produced by Gil Brealey; directed by Oliver Howes. Learning Corporation of America, 1982, c1981. Videocassette: 28 minutes. VHS.

Examines Japanese industry and takes a closer look at individual participation in Japan's gigantic economy. Shows the pros and cons of Japan's paternalistic capitalism and the underlying fragility of the economy. (Gr. 9-12)

Made in Japan, Part I: Cultural Differences on Industry. Madison, WI: Produced by MTI, 1982. Videocassette, color, 16 minutes.

A penetrating analysis of the Japanese industrial economy. Investigates a modern-day economic miracle and compares it with the plight of the American system. (Gr. 7+)

Understanding the Japanese Economy. Eau Claire, WI: Center for Economic Education, Videocassette, color, 28 minutes.

Discusses Japanese education, international relations, and the structure of the Japanese corporation. Topics include juko schools, lifetime employment, decision making, quality control circles, and internationalization. (Gr. 9-12)

Beyond the Rising Sun: Discovering Japan, by Michael Roessler, 1985.
Decision-making about Japanese family values is explored through simulation. Students' success depends on how well they come to understand the principles of Japanese society. Designed for junior high through adult levels. For use with Apple II, II+, IIe/48k/disk drive, BASIC. Available from:
Educational Activities
P.O. Box 392
Freeport, NY 11520
Price: $69.00

Shogun Showdown, by Michael Roessler, 1984.
Software with a television game show format: questions on culture, economics, recreation, and land. Suitable for pre- and post-unit testing. Questions offer two levels of difficulty with imaginary awards for correct answers. Designed for use by one or two players at the junior high level. For use with Apple II or Apple II-e. Available from:
Mike Roessler
611 James Street
Portland, MI 48875
Price: $5.00 (may be copied)

Japanese Government Offices in the United States

Consulate General of Japan
737 North Michigan Avenue
Suite 1100
Chicago, IL 50511
(312) 280-0400

The Embassy of Japan
2520 Massachusetts Avenue, N.W.
Washington, D.C. 20008
(202) 234-2266

Permanent Mission of Japan to the
United Nations
866 United Nations Plaza
New York, NY 10017
(202) 421-9580

Japanese Organizations

Japan Air Lines (JAL)
225 North Michigan Avenue
Chicago, Illinois 60601

Japan American Society of Chicago, Inc.
36 South Wabash Avenue
Chicago, Illinois 60603

Japan America Society of Minnesota, Inc.
6101 Halefox Avenue So.
Edina, Minnesota 55424

Japan Economic Institute
1000 Connecticut Avenue, N.W.
Washington, D.C. 20036
(202) 296-5633

Japan External Trade Organization
1200 17th Street, Suite 141
Denver, Colorado 80202

Japan External Trade Organization
(JETRO)
401 North Michigan Avenue, Suite 660
Chicago, Illinois 60611
(312) 527-9000

Japan Information Center
Consulate General of Japan
153 East 53rd Street
New York, NY 10022

Japan National Tourist Organization
333 North Michigan Avenue
Chicago, Illinois 60601
(312) 332-3975

Japan Society
Education Department
333 East 47th Street
New York, NY 10017
(212) 832-1155

Japanese Chamber of Commerce and
  Industry
230 North Michigan Avenue
Suite 2108
Chicago, Illinois 60601
(312) 332-6199

Educational Organizations

Katherine Pierson
Asia Resources Center
University of Missouri-St. Louis
SSBE Tower, 8001 Natural Bridge Road
St. Louis, MO 63121

The Asia Society
Education and Communication Department
725 Park Avenue
New York, NY 10021
(212) 288-6400

Bureau of Audio-Visual Instruction (BAVI)
P.O. Box 2093
Madison, WI 53701-2093
Telephone: 1-800-362-6888

Center for Asian Studies
University of Illinois
1208 West California
Urbana, Illinois 61801
(217) 333-4850

Center for East Asian Studies
University of Wisconsin
1440 Van Hise Hall
Madison, WI 53706
(608) 262-7801

Japan Economic Institute
1000 Connecticut Avenue, N.W.
Washington, D.C. 20036
(202) 296-5633

Japan External Trade Organization
1200 17th Street, Suite 141
Denver, Colorado 80202

Center for Economic Education
c/o Dr. Jerry D. Johnson
University of Wisconsin-Eau Claire
Eau Claire, WI 54701

East Asian Curriculum Project
Columbia University
420 West 118th Street
New York, NY 10027
(212) 280-4278

East Asia Resource Center
Thompson Hall DR-05
University of Washington
Seattle, WA 98195
(206) 543-1921

East Asian Studies Center
Indiana University
205 Memorial Hall West
Bloomington, Indiana 47405
(812) 335-3765

Films Incorporated
5547 North Ravenswood Avenue
Chicago, Illinois 60640-1199
Telephone: (800) 323-4222, Ext. 43

Great Lakes-Japan in the Schools Program
College of Education
152 Pillsbury Drive, S.E.
University of Minnesota
Minneapolis, Minnesota 55455
(612) 626-0555

Japan Project: SPICE
Lou Henry Hoover Building
Stanford University
Stanford, California 94305
(415) 497-1114

Japanese American Curriculum Project
c/o Paul Yoshiwara
414 Third Avenue
San Mateo, California 94401
(415) 343-9408

Japan Program Services
University of Wisconsin-Eau Claire
Schofield Hall 111
Eau Claire, WI 54703
(715) 836-3847

Learning Corporation of America
1350 Avenue of the Americas
New York, New York 10019

The Midwest Program for
    Teaching About Japan
Indiana University
2805 East 10th Street
Bloomington, IN 47405
(812) 335-3838

The National Council for the Social Studies
3501 Newark Street, N.W.
Washington, D.C. 20016
(202) 966-7840

Office of Multicultural and
    Equity Education
Old Capitol Building, FG-11
Olympic, WA 98504
(206) 753-2560

Social Studies Development Center
Indiana University
2805 East 10th Street
Room 120
Bloomington, Indiana 47405
(815) 335-3838

University of Tennessee
Research Corp. (information)
Communications Building, Suite 415
University of Tennessee
Knoxville, TN 37996-0344

Center for Economic Education (rental)
205 Founders Hall
University of Tennessee
Chattanooga, TN 37403

Publishers and Bookstores

American Bookstore (For K-12 catalog)
c/o Charlotte Murakami
321 Towne Avenue
Los Angeles, CA 90013
(213) 680-2888

Charles E. Tuttle, Inc.
28 South Main Street
P.O. Box 140
Rutland, Vermont 85701
(802) 773-8930
(Also publishes Weatherhill books)

Japanese American Curriculum Project
(JACP)
414 East Third Avenue
San Mateo, CA 94401
(415) 343-9408

Kinokuni-ya Bookstore of America
1581 Webster
San Francisco, CA 94115
(415) 567-7625

Kodansha International
10 East 53rd Street
New York, NY 10022
(212) 393-7050

Pen Pal Organizations

Afro-Asian Pen Pal Center
Robert Carroll, Director
CPO
P.O. Box 337
Saugerties, NY 12477

International Pen-Friend Association
(Kokusai Pen Furendo Kyokai)
19-7, Oosugi 1-chome
Edogawa, Tokyo 132
Japan
Telephone: 03-816-6526

Japan Pen Pal's League
CPO Box 121
Okayama 700-91
Japan

Nippon Yubin Tomonokai Kyokai
5-16, Yushima 4-chome
Bunkyo, Tokyo 113
Japan
Telephone: 03-816-6526